HOW TO DESIGN, DEVELOP, AND MARKET HEALTH CARE SEMINARS

Ronald J. Friedman, PhD

Penny Altman, MA

Professional Resource Press
Sarasota, Florida

Published by
Professional Resource Press
(An imprint of the Professional Resource Exchange, Inc.)
Post Office Box 15560
Sarasota, FL 34277-1560

Printed in the United States of America

Copyright © 1997 by Professional Resource Exchange, Inc.

All rights reserved

No part of this book may be reproduced, stored in a retrieval system, or transmitted, in any form or by any means, either electronic, mechanical, photocopying, microfilming, recording, or otherwise, without written permission from the publisher.

The copy editor was David Anson, the managing editor was Debra Fink, the production coordinator was Laurie Girsch, and the cover designer was Carol Tornatore.

Library of Congress Cataloging-in-Publication Data

Friedman, Ronald J., date.
    How to design, develop, and market health care seminars / Ronald
J. Friedman, Penny Altman
        p.   cm.
    Includes bibliographical references and index.
    ISBN 1-56887-029-9 (alk. paper)
    1. Medicine--Study and teaching (Continuing education)--Handbooks,
manuals, etc.   2. Health education--Handbooks, manuals, etc.
    3. Workshops (Adult education)--Handbooks, manuals, etc.
    4. Seminars--Handbooks, manuals, etc.   I. Altman, Penny, date.
    II. Title.
    R845.F75   1997
    362.1'068'8--dc21   97-16166
                                                                          CIP

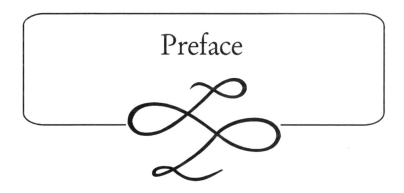

Preface

We never intended to write a book about developing and marketing seminars. Nor did we know that so many people were interested in presenting seminars of their own. However, a number of people who had attended our seminars expressed interest in our work and asked how they could go about developing and marketing their own programs.

Through informal discussion and consultation, we helped several people overcome the obstacles that kept them from getting started and we helped others expand small programs into larger seminars. A few people had well-developed topics; others needed assistance defining subjects for their seminars. Everyone had questions about marketing and the logistics of setting up meeting sites, obtaining mailing lists, and, probably most significant of all, determining whether they were on the right track before they invested money in their projects.

Most of those who attended our programs were professionals with limited business experience so all these questions raised enough doubt in their minds to keep most of them from taking the first steps toward producing successful seminars. In time, we became convinced that many people have good ideas and could be enthusiastic seminar presenters if we could help them get past the initial obstacles inherent in their indecision and fear of the unknown.

We helped with basic market research and, using our own experience, showed people how to begin with modest start-up costs. We knew that many seminars could be advertised and promoted for an initial outlay of $500 or less. It excited us when a number of people decided to give it a try using our help. Although we had built up quite a bit of seminar experience of our own by that time, the idea for this book grew primarily out of working with others. We learned even more as we helped them solve their development, design, and marketing problems.

How to Design, Develop, and Market Health Care Seminars will help you explore your own ideas for topics and then guide you step-by-step through each stage of the seminar development and marketing process, including the successful presentation of your program. Finally, we will help you evaluate your seminar, fine tune it, and use it as a stepping stone to other rewarding projects.

We followed different paths to the seminar business, which now occupies us full-time. Ron Friedman was a clinical psychologist with a busy practice, who had built much of his practice by offering seminars and workshops. Penny Altman had worked in organizational development. She had extensive experience working with business leaders and managers. We have found the seminar business stimulating, demanding, exciting, and rewarding. We think you will find it equally so.

Call us if you have questions or would like to let us know how the ideas in this book worked for you.

RJF and PA

Table of Contents

HOW TO DESIGN, DEVELOP, AND MARKET HEALTH CARE SEMINARS

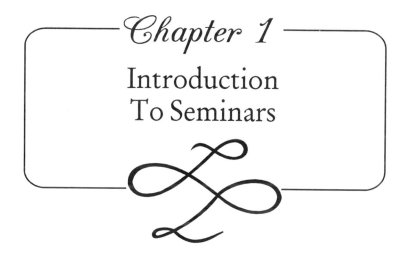

Chapter 1
Introduction
To Seminars

Seminars and workshops are big business. Since 1990, the fastest growing area in education has been providing professional and technical workers with upgraded knowledge and skills (Johnson, 1995). Professional journals and magazines are filled with advertisements for professional development seminars, personal growth workshops, self-improvement courses, and surveys of new scientific developments. And in churches, schools, hospitals, post offices, community centers, libraries, and grocery stores across the country, bulletin boards are cluttered with announcements of more seminars, workshops, courses, and study groups.

The best estimates suggest that business and industry spend nearly 50 billion dollars a year on educational programs. The personal growth market adds another 12 to 15 billion dollars while continuing education, professional updates, and general interest programs in medical fields contribute an additional 20 billion dollars. In fact, there are so many lectures, seminars, and workshops we have to ask, is there room for more? In our experience, there is always a place for another course or seminar. But, there is room only if new programs meet two important criteria: They must be of high quality; and they have to be marketed carefully, targeted at groups of people who will find them sufficiently interesting to take the time and pay the tuition necessary to attend.

In this book, we will help you choose topics for your programs, identify niches where you can find an audience, and develop marketing plans to sell your seminars. Once your program is ready, we will guide you through its presentation and evaluation in order to improve and refine your work. Finally, we will help you look back at your efforts from different perspectives to learn how to modify successful programs for new audiences and different markets.

The seminar business is exciting and dynamic. It provides an opportunity to add a new dimension to your professional activities. In addition, presenting seminars can bring a great deal of personal satisfaction along with a welcome boost to your income. The remarkable growth of seminars and short training courses over the past few years is not a passing fad. Rather, growth is likely to continue at an accelerating rate. This growth will come from changes taking place in how most of us will work in the last few years of this century and the early part of the next.

These changes are not speculation; they are already fact. The average size of U.S. companies as measured by number of employees is shrinking. More people are in business for themselves or part of small businesses and partnerships. Technical workers, often very well paid, are replacing blue collar manufacturing workers. Even in medicine and allied health fields where the trend in many areas seems to be toward bigger and less personal organizations, almost everyone, from the ground up, already feels pressure - that will only increase - to specialize and present himself or herself with a marketable package of skills. There will be tremendous pressure on individual practitioners to be complete unto themselves if they are to carve out a professionally satisfying role in health care. In medicine and allied fields, we are experiencing phenomenal growth with a greater number of jobs, some of which are basic service-level jobs, but more and more require not only a sophisticated level of entry skills but the need to avail oneself of constant updates and continuing professional education.

Walter Kiechel, writing in *Fortune* (1993), listed six trends that will reshape everyone's workplace. Two we have already noted.

1. The average company will become smaller, employing fewer people. While providers of health care will continue to see the unit size increase, the number of professional people per patient or client will continue to decline.
2. The traditional hierarchical organization we are used to in business and the professions will give way to a variety of organizational forms, the network of specialists foremost among them.
3. Technicians, ranging from computer repairpersons to radiation therapists, will replace manufacturing operatives as the worker elite.
4. The vertical division of labor will be replaced by a horizontal division.
5. The paradigm of doing business will shift from making a product to providing a service.
6. Work itself will be redefined: constant learning, more high-order thinking, less nine-to-five.

Add to this list the increased isolation of people in small offices or working from their homes and you can see the vast potential for a growth industry, providing the training, updating, and reviewing that all of these workers and professionals will need.

The pace of change in technical and professional areas is breathtaking. The rate of information growth is staggering. Most people will not have the time, inclination, or ability to absorb everything they need or want to know unless it is provided for them in a readily digestible form. Much of this information will arrive along the information highways. And much of it will come from seminars and short courses of the type discussed here.

By the time the new century dawns, readers of this book will be participants in many such programs, certainly as learners and possibly as teachers. The formats and modalities through which the programs will be delivered will vary markedly. Will your audience consist of 100 people in a conference room? A thousand people who bought your new videotape with interactive features? Or thousands more who learn from the digitally stored programs available through fiber optic connections with your electronic office? Or will they sit back in a comfortable chair and read your book? Maybe a little of them all.

Changes in how we work will open opportunities for anyone interested in taking advantage of them. An increase in seminars and workshops is part of the inevitable change.

WHAT IS A SEMINAR?

A seminar is usually a short course on a limited subject. Most of our seminars are 1-day programs, but we offer 2- and 3-day seminars as well. Typically, a seminar is a lecture or demonstration. This type of seminar is distinct from college seminars where a small group of advanced students and their teacher do a great deal of outside reading and then meet for discussion. The expectation people have for the seminars discussed here is that they will come and listen and we will either talk or demonstrate examples of the topic in question. In addition, in a seminar people usually expect a "how to" orientation. They come not just to learn facts or gain some interesting information; usually they expect to be able to use what they have learned in their daily lives or professional work.

We use the words seminar and workshop almost interchangeably, but some people make a distinction. For some a workshop implies more active participation by the audience. We will use the term workshop to extend the meaning of the seminar just a little bit. For example, we often encourage brief discussions between members of the audience, and we expand question and answer sessions by looking to the audience for additional comments.

WHAT ARE YOUR GOALS?

Before you take another step, you should take time to decide what you hope to accomplish with your plans for a seminar. For some, the goal is to attract attention to special skills and experience that will serve as an aid to build a professional practice. For others, the appeal is primarily supplemental income. Others like to teach. For others still, the goal is variety, a change from the routines of the office or hospital ward, but a change that still allows them to practice their profession and take advantage of knowledge gained from many years of study and work. Of course, you can have more than one goal. You can also have a hierarchy of goals. Perhaps you have said, "Let's see how it goes. If I can develop this and make a success of it, maybe I can take the show on the road. If not, I will be happy with a boost to my practice or the change in scenery the seminars allow me."

Usually people have a pretty good notion of what they want to do and why they want to do it. But developing and marketing a seminar is a business for many of us and, if it is going to be a business for you, it has to be approached like one. Physicians, psychologists, nurses, physical therapists, social workers, educators, speech pathologists, audiologists, and other professionals who are trained as practitioners are, as a rule, not experienced in business, and their lack of familiarity with notions such as business plans and marketing strategies, as well as more fundamental issues such as cost accounting, dooms some ambitious and wonderful projects before they ever get off the ground.

Throughout this book our emphasis will be to help you accomplish all that is needed to launch your seminar with a minimum of effort and cost, so we don't suggest that you need a business degree or to hire an accountant right away. But we do want to stress the point that if you think you are going to do more than add a little variety to your professional life or your goals are to go beyond just building your practice, you ought to recognize that you are launching a business and that your skills as a professional, even one experienced in running a professional office, may need to be supplemented. If, at the outset, you have a clear idea of your goals, many of the decisions you will have to make will flow naturally, including where you will hold the seminar, how much money you are willing to invest in it, how much you will have to charge, and how much effort you are willing to put in.

FOUR GOOD REASONS TO PRESENT SEMINARS

As an Aid to Marketing

Whether you are marketing a professional practice, selling books and materials, or marketing yourself in a consulting business, seminars can be very effective. They are especially powerful at attracting patients and clients to your professional practice and helping sell material you have published or produced. Potential clients or patients have an opportunity to see you in action and determine for themselves if you meet their needs. You have a chance to put your best foot forward and, without boasting, pull out all the stops to show your audience how knowledgeable or understanding you can be. Free seminars generate interest in your professional practice, but even seminars for which you charge a registration fee and/or sell materials can be a rich source of interest in you and your practice.

Not only individuals offer seminars, but today's competitive marketplace demands that hospitals, clinics, public agencies, and practice groups of all kinds use seminars to promote themselves, too. Most hospitals have marketing and public relations departments that utilize lectures, seminars, and workshops as the backbone of their promotion efforts. In many cases the seminar is not set up to make a profit. Many seminars are offered free. The intent is to gain an introduction to the audience, secure a higher profile in the community, and interest people who attend in a product or service. Free seminars offer rich opportunities. Seminars enable the physician, psychologist, or social worker who has opened a new office to build a practice or allow the experienced practitioner an opportunity to highlight a new specialty. Free seminars usually qualify for free advertising in newspapers and on radio stations or the use of public facilities such as school gymnasiums, lecture rooms, church meeting halls or basements, or community college lecture rooms, all of which keep your costs low. Free programs are often viewed as community service even when they also serve your business interests.

Medical institutions, physicians, and other health care providers can use seminars to address issues related to managed care. With the increase of managed care systems for all aspects of health care, many practitioners have seen portions of their practices disappear as large segments of their patients become captives of preferred provider groups or health maintenance organizations. Seminars allow you to highlight your practice. People in the community can meet you and get to know you. This will influence some of them when they choose a physician who may not be part of their panel of providers or who has a highly specialized skill or interest that they think they need. Even when this involves some financial sacrifice on the part of the patient, if he or she is convinced you are the best or only resource, it is one more way to build a practice.

Produce Supplemental Income

Depending on your interest and commitment, seminars can contribute a substantial amount of money to your income. Promoting and presenting seminars is a lot like freelance writing. You can do a little on the side as a hobby, or you can do a lot of it, but still work at another job. For some, however, it becomes a full-time job with the goal to produce and present seminars as a source of full-time income and personal satisfaction. One of the premier advantages of the seminar business is the high degree of job satisfaction that most people in the business have. This is true for those who do it only part time as well.

Introduce Variety Into Your Professional Life

No matter what work they do, most people like a little variety. You might want a change of scenery or some relief from tasks you do on a routine basis. Seminars are outstanding vehicles for this purpose. Seminars allow you to pursue an interesting topic to an extent your usual busy life does not allow and give you a chance to enjoy the travel that is often a fringe benefit of presenting seminars. For example, once a year, in November or December, we offer a half-day program on one of our more popular topics in Honolulu. We go a day or 2 early and, after the seminar, fly to one of the other Hawaiian islands and spend an extra 3 or 4 days. It is a delightful way to combine business and pleasure with a vacation more than paid for by the work we do. If these were not busy months in the seminar business we would stay longer.

Provide an Opportunity to Teach

Many professionals enjoy teaching and would do more of it if they could. But opportunities to teach in colleges and universities are limited and, when they do occur, demand a commitment over an extended period of time and to a schedule that is often incompatible with the demands of a busy professional. Setting up your own seminars can give you the opportunity to teach about what you like, interact with your students or audience in any fashion that pleases you, and still provide the good feelings most of us get when we teach a course or lesson that we know is interesting and well received.

TWO REASONS TO HESITATE
BEFORE OFFERING SEMINARS

Cost

Although seminars can be initiated with only a modest outlay of money, often even elaborate programs can be undertaken for $500 or less. You must also take into consideration the time you spend developing the program in calculating your cost. But many people find the time invested a labor of love and regard it the same as the time they would invest in a hobby.

Time and Attention Diverted
From Your Primary Job

In our experience, the sacrifice of time needed to get a seminar rolling, while substantial, is not the main sacrifice. Rather, for many people, all their creative energy flows into the seminar, and that can detract from the attention given to daily work. This is not a scientific business. This is an issue that you have to decide for yourself. It is usually not a serious problem as long as you recognize what can happen.

CHARACTERISTICS OF
GOOD SEMINARS

Think back to the last seminar that you enjoyed and found useful. What were the characteristics of that program that made it so? At the same time, recall a program you attended that did not live up to your expectations. Why not? What was it about this disappointing seminar that caused it to fail? Undoubtedly, the content of the program - the facts you learned or did not learn - played an important role in your reaction to the seminar and in determining its value to you. But it is just as likely the content of the program was not the only feature of the seminar that determined whether you would attend a similar program in the future presented by the same instructor or sponsoring body.

There are a number of characteristics that define a good or successful program:

1. *Was the knowledge level appropriate for the audience?* It takes careful planning to make sure the content of a seminar is appropriate for your audience even when the audience is similar in professional training and background. But, usually, most of us find a heterogeneous audience facing us when we stand up to speak. When we present seminars based on the content of this book, some people attend with a clear seminar topic in mind while others have only a vague idea or none at all. Some members of

the audience will have completed preliminary market research to assess interest in their topic; others will not even know what market research is. A portion of the audience will have good ideas about how to sell their seminar; others will have none. We have to meet the needs of them all. In addition, people who attend any seminar differ, not only in prior knowledge about the seminar topic, reason for being in the audience that day, and particular interests, but they may have widely differing expectations. No matter how hard you try to attract a homogeneous audience you will always face a mixed group. That does not have to be a serious problem. You have probably been to programs with others whose interests differed from yours, but your own needs were met satisfactorily. Still, it takes extra effort to prepare for a diverse audience. Herman Holtz, in his book *Expanding Your Consulting Practice With Seminars* (1987), offers the example of the effort he made to advertise an "advanced" seminar on proposal writing. Novices were explicitly warned away and the message was repeated several times in the advertising copy. Nonetheless, Holtz says he wound up with audiences that usually were comprised of better than 50% beginners no matter what he did. So his solution was to adapt the seminar to accommodate the reality. We all have to do that. Nonetheless, the audience has the right to expect the seminar leader to present most of the material at a level useful for them.

2. *Was the seminar well organized with a proper amount of material?* The quantity of material presented must fit the time and structure of the seminar. It must be well organized. Too little material, even if interesting and useful, spread over too much time, will cause frustration or boredom. If material is presented in a way that is not compatible with the content itself (e.g., incomplete case illustrations or skills merely described rather than demonstrated), it will seem peripheral to participants. On the other hand, there is a limit to what even a highly motivated, intelligent learner can absorb in a fixed period of time. If you are

overly eager and provide too much material to make sure you cover everything, you risk overwhelming your audience. They will be unable to keep everything organized or in perspective. They won't be able to sort the wheat from the chaff. They may leave thinking about a variety of different points while the main issues, integration of the material, or synthesis of ideas may suffer. In any case, participants will have the subjective feeling, even if they cannot identify it clearly in their own minds, that the program was not satisfying or did not meet their expectations even if you have provided a wealth of information.

Efforts at organization should not be obvious, but the results should be. Did the program flow smoothly? Was there a logical consistency in the flow of information? Did the learner have the background necessary from his or her own experience or earlier portions of the program to make sense of what came later? Was the design good? Was there sufficient variation in presentation style or material to maintain interest? Did the design of the seminar help or hinder the audience's ability to concentrate and get the maximum benefit from the experience?

3. *Were supplemental and handout materials relevant and useful?* It is easy to print bibliographies, reprints of journal articles, and lists of conference attendees along with other material that make a handsome package but get tossed away rather than used. For reasons we will probably never know, many people who attend seminars like to walk away with handout material. That's fine if it supplements or complements the program and is likely to be used. If it is nothing more than summaries of material presented or has no practical application it may leave members of your audience feeling they did not get what they came for - even if they might have been satisfied with a good program and no handouts at all.

4. *Did the presenter seem committed to the seminar topic?* You can tell if a teacher cares about the material being taught. As a member of the audience, you want to be certain the seminar leader not only shares your interest in the topic, but is sufficiently committed to its study or

practice to have put in the time to understand it well. This ensures the presenter is able to go beyond superficial or common knowledge and add either additional learning or his or her own passionately held views that should prove stimulating in one way or another for you.

5. *Was the seminar material timely?* Most of us have attended a lecture or seminar only to find we knew most of the material presented by the "experts." That's not all bad. In fact, the experience can make you feel pretty good about yourself. But the good feeling goes only a small way if you have given up a whole day of work to attend a program that repeats old information or rehashes things you already know. Being timely refers not only to up-to-the-minute scientific study results, but timeliness also includes current mainstream thinking and theoretical formulations. So if you attend a program that presents familiar old data but gives them a new twist or interpretation or raises new questions that stimulate your own thinking, that is timely too.

6. *Did the seminar meet your expectations?* There are many ways to present the same material. Brochures and other promotional material explain what will be presented in the seminar and for what type of audience the seminar is intended. That's a contract. Were the terms of the contract met? Did you get what you expected? Was it presented in a way that was useful for you?

7. *Was the price reasonable?* Most people are pretty sophisticated consumers. They know when they have been overcharged, and they recognize it can occur in different ways. You can charge too much - even for an excellent program - so people walk away with a grudging feeling that the seminar was not worth the cost. Or you can overcharge, even with a small fee, if your audience does not feel they got what they paid for. In any community it is easy to find out what different types of programs sell for. Price makes a difference.

8. *Was the setting comfortable and appropriate?* The location of a 90-minute program is less important than that for

a full day, but even short programs have to be set in a place consistent with your purpose. If your primary purpose is educational, you can use a church basement with folding chairs for an hour and a half or use the school gym or library. If you are trying to build your practice you might be better off in a warmer setting such as your office conference room or waiting room or a moderate size meeting room in a local hotel. Make people comfortable, and make the setting fit your purpose.

9. *Was the length of the program reasonable?* No one likes marathon programs, especially those that do not begin and end on time. If you say you will start at 9:00, then start at 9:00. If you start 5 minutes late because latecomers cannot find parking places tell your early arrivals, before 9:00, why you will be delayed. They will not be angry as long as you explain. Then stick to your schedule. It shows you respect the people who paid to hear you and care that they have fit your program into an otherwise busy schedule. The length of the program has to fit the content, too. Most laymen have little interest in a program that lasts more than an hour and a half or so. Professional updates in most fields can be presented in a 30- to 90-minute frame. But most people expect continuing education programs and workshops and seminars that teach skills to last longer.

PLAN FOR THE FUTURE

It may seem premature to begin a discussion of planning for the future before the end of the first chapter of this book, but in the seminar business, as in most areas of human endeavor, you will benefit in the long run if you set out with at least a rough idea of where you want to end up. If you have ever created anything in the arts, business, or your profession, you know that the finished product usually did look exactly as you had envisioned before you began your journey.

Somewhere along the way ideas take on a life of their own, and the struggle to create becomes, in many ways, a learning process as you create as well as observe what is developing. And you must not fear such an experience. Many professional people have a hard time surrendering absolute control even if it is only to another part of themselves, their creative side. Sometimes you have to let things develop and see what comes about.

There should be a general path you want your seminar or workshop to follow, but there are other ideas that will arise in the course of development and when you present your program. If you are overwhelmed by these new ideas or see them as distractions instead of opportunities, you may lose sight of alternative paths you can follow after the core of your seminar is developed.

When we first got started in the seminar business, we were concerned about getting programs designed and sold and had little patience or even thoughts about anything else. We developed some excellent programs and some that were not quite so good. We marketed as aggressively and as intelligently as we could, and most of our programs were personally satisfying and financially successful - but by no means all of them. After the intensity that characterized the early stages of development and presentation diminished, scarcely a day went by that we didn't think of modifications, extensions, juxtapositions, and other revisions that spawned a host of new ideas that took us into new areas again and again.

So we look at the development of seminars as a dynamic process that yields changes over time and unfolds from within itself to develop new ideas and programs. Nurture this dynamic process. Keep your enthusiasm and interest high so that the spark of creativity and joy that gives rise to the first of your endeavors remains to animate what comes later. And, because interests and fads and competition keep changing the features of the competitive landscape, the evolving nature of your own work will keep you going with new material and interests. In this way your workshop business need not be limited to a single topic or a brief time period but can become an important part of your professional activities.

Chapter 2

Selecting a
Topic for Your Seminar

The purpose of your program will have a substantial influence on your seminar topic. Is your seminar for a general audience? Or are you going to translate some fundamental information from your profession for a group of allied professionals? For example, you may be a psychiatrist offering seminars for psychologists and social workers on the use of antidepressant or antianxiety medications. Or you may offer seminars for your psychiatric colleagues on recent advances in some aspect of treatment or diagnosis that you recently learned at a postgraduate seminar. Is your seminar on Alzheimer's disease for family practice physicians or specialists, such as neurologists or gerontologists? Perhaps, instead, you want to talk to families of patients with the disease or the nursing staff in a residential care facility. Or, maybe, at different times, you hope to address them all.

There is no prepackaged set of lecture notes you can take off the shelf and read to your seminar audience. Decisions about the content of a seminar as well as format and organization, choice of what to include or exclude, what to assume the audience already knows, and what you will have to teach, all play a part in choosing your seminar topic. The main topic is important, but so is choosing the proper angle that will capture your audience. The same topic often lends itself to many different treatments and serves different audiences.

FINDING TOPIC IDEAS

The best seminars arise from topics in which the seminar leader has great interest or feels great passion. If you already have an idea for a seminar, it probably developed from some aspect of your profession. You know the subject well and think others might want to know about it, too. You may be certain there is interest in your topic because patients or clients ask about it every day. Or you may be a child psychologist who realizes there are thousands of teachers or child care workers who should know certain information in order to work effectively with the children they serve.

Perhaps your geriatric or psychiatric practice has taught you about the needs of children of older adults or the information lacking among people who provide their care in adult day care, retirement, or nursing homes. It may be that your experience in forensic psychiatry has let you see first hand the needs of prison corrections officers or juvenile court workers, and you know you can fill those needs. Or, as a physical therapist, you not only have a pretty good understanding about why people frequently fail to follow through with treatment programs, but your study and experience have made you an expert on medical compliance which is applicable in many areas of medical care.

And you may have public speaking experience already. Perhaps you have been interviewed by a newspaper or television reporter. You might have written for lay or professional publications. It's unlikely you would be reading this book if you had not already given a fair amount of thought to the possibility of presenting a seminar and even to what you might present.

On the other hand, many people have never given serious thought to presenting a seminar beyond the passing notion that they would like to give it a try. For many, the difficulty formulating a specific topic serves as a barrier to carrying the idea further. Or, in still another circumstance, someone with a terrific idea may lack the basic, practical information needed to put the idea into operation.

You may already have an idea for your seminar. If not, there are many ways to generate topics. Leave aside for the moment the very important question of how to tell if your idea is a good idea and will attract an audience. Do not let doubts and second guessing paralyze you to the extent that your uncertainty prevents you from taking the next step in developing your seminar. Of course, it is important to choose a topic that will work, but it is just as important to realize that there is no way to be absolutely certain of success. It is hard to be confident doing something you have never tried before. So if you, like so many people, refuse to take the next step until you are absolutely certain that all will work out perfectly, you will never take anything but the most cautious uninventive steps. There are usually more arguments against doing something new or creative than there are in favor of doing it. There are always plenty of people who seem happy to point out the flaws in your idea or tell you why a particular strategy won't work, or is too complex, or is too expensive, or has already been tried many times and failed. Listen to the naysayers at your peril.

It is not that the critical evaluation of your idea is not important; of course it is. It is just that if you allow your critical faculty to hold sway too early in the creative process, it will dampen the fires of your creativity and raise the level of your uncertainty and doubt so high that you are unlikely to push on.

"Banish the Critic." Post those words over the desk where you work or write. Keep the critic in your head away from the work you do early in the game. Get your ideas out. Put your thoughts on paper (or on your hard drive). But get them out where you and others can look at them. There will be plenty of time to sort the wheat from the chaff later on. A badly expressed concept or poorly written sentence can be critically examined later. The idea you censor before it has a chance to be expressed at all can never be objectively evaluated or refined or even recognized for how wonderful it really is or could be with a little work. Banish the critic for now.

Use the Exercise for Selecting Topics on pages 43-44 if you do not have a seminar idea in mind, but try it even if you are sure you know exactly what you want to do. Keep this worksheet as a reference as we discuss topic selection further.

Right now would be a good time to abandon the fantasy that there is one perfect topic for you or one perfect topic that is timely right now and most likely to capture an audience. If you dither about choosing a topic, you are just stalling, and you have to figure out why you are stalling in order to move ahead. The reason for your delay certainly is not the lack of interesting or timely topics or even your inability to deliver them. The best way to defeat doubt, anxiety, or all the other causes of hesitation and inaction is to follow the fundamentals as we outline them in this book.

MARKET RESEARCH

Market research can be elaborate and formal, but most of the market research we use is informal and inexpensive. Different forms of market research are appropriate for different types of questions and situations, so we will discuss market research in some detail. No matter how delightful your topic, no matter how wonderful you are as a speaker or teacher, some research will be necessary as you develop your topic. Research will help you refine and focus a topic you already have and will also help define new topics or different dimensions of the topic you have in mind. Do not skip market research as a way to save time or a few dollars. Carefully thought out market research is always worth its cost. You may be surprised to learn you have done some research already. But even more elaborate research need not consume a lot of time or money.

Look around you. Perhaps you never thought of looking around as market research, but it is. What do you read or watch on TV or talk to people about that suggests topics? What are the hot topics? What are the topics of enduring interest in newspapers and magazines that are related to your professional knowledge or interests? Look at the competition. See what the adult education programs in your community offer or what your local college or university has on its continuing education schedule. What are you reading in your professional journals? Are there adaptations for a lay audience? Adaptations for a professional audience? Do you have a specialty or subspecialty interest your general practicing colleagues might find interesting?

Herman Holtz, who has taught the development of seminars and other presentations in his own books and seminars, has listed 10 useful questions to guide the development of your idea (Holtz, 1987). Based on Holtz's work, we have created 10 questions of our own angled toward our needs. Review these questions periodically while developing your program. They will stimulate creative thought. In most cases we will assume you are perusing a medical or mental health topic; usually, but not always, it is a clinical topic.

1. What are the two or three questions your patients or clients ask about your topic?
2. What complaints do you hear? Which elements of the problem or management of the problem cause them the most frustration? Which of these are complaints inherent in the problem and which come from other people's inability to meet their needs?
3. What do these people say are the most important problems or the ones that cause them the greatest frustration for not being met?
4. Do these questions and complaints seem sensible and realistic to you given what you know about the issue?
5. What special knowledge or experience do you have that you could apply to these questions?
6. What other seminars are being offered to your target market or related markets?
7. What could you do differently that would set your seminar apart?
8. Is there an aspect of your knowledge, experience, or view of the topic or your background that would let you find a

special angle that would be different than others are presenting?
9.   Does your perspective on the topic suggest any special
     niches or different groups of people who might be inter-
     ested aside from the obvious target market?
10. Can you present your material or seminar in a way that
     makes it special or stand out from what others present?

You will not be able to give definitive answers to all of these
questions at first, but they will serve as a guide to keep you on
track as you develop your seminar. Just as important, the responses you give now to these questions compared to the answers
you will give later will give you confidence as you validate your
own judgment about the value of what you have to offer.

We assume that the topic for your first or current seminar has
grown or will develop from your own interest or specialty. It is
certainly possible to start from scratch and learn all that is necessary to present a successful seminar. Or you can hire someone
with good credentials to present the program. As an alternative,
you can invite several people to speak and reserve for yourself the
role of organizer or promoter. But the focus in this book will
remain on topics that develop from your own knowledge, interest,
or professional training.

In addition, we will operate on the assumption that the reader
would prefer (or has) to do the job as inexpensively as possible.
You can spend a lot of money setting up seminars, and there are
some circumstances when it might be necessary. But for the most
part careful planning is a good substitute for spending a lot of
money. Of course, if you are fortunate enough to develop a
program that immediately grosses tens of thousands of dollars, a
few extra dollars for postage and the addition of a third attractive
color to your brochure may not be much of a problem. But we
have found that most people have little experience and are starting
from scratch without even knowing whether they will be able to
pull it off. Under these circumstances no one wants to put a lot
of money at risk, especially when it is not necessary.

And there is no need to sacrifice quality to save money. It is
easy to buy a mailing list, hire a designer to prepare a flyer, and

then turn the whole project over to a commercial mailing house to distribute your material and charge $5,000. What takes planning and careful thought is doing the same job on a shoestring budget.

USING ADVISORY COMMITTEES TO HELP DEVELOP SEMINAR TOPICS

Advisory committees exist to give advice, of course, but used creatively, they can be a rich source of ideas you could never come up with on your own. We use advisory committees primarily for brainstorming sessions, asking them to take our ideas and critique them, extend them, or extrapolate from them in any way they like. No matter how many times we have done this, by the time the process runs its course, we are still amazed at the different angles and points of view that can be brought to bear on a topic. This is true even with topics where we already regard ourselves as experts.

There are two ways to staff advisory committees. The first is to compose a committee of colleagues, friends, or even family members, who know you and your work. Make sure you include people able to give you an objective point of view of your strengths and weaknesses, people who are not afraid to tell you what they think. Even with friends or co-workers it is best to add some formality to the advisory process. Give each individual a clear idea of what you would like them to do. Explain what you are looking for and tell them what kind of information you would like them to provide. Write it down. Finding a careful balance between providing too much structure that might inhibit creative exchanges among your advisors and leaving so much ambiguity that they cannot do their job takes careful thought. Allow several days or a week for them to think about what you want them to do, and then get everyone together for a brainstorming session. Schedule just one session of about 90 minutes. That's enough. You will get more than 90 minutes of their time. In the days and weeks after the meeting, you will receive suggestions and ideas as everyone continues to think more about what was discussed.

Your presence at the meeting may inhibit an open flow of ideas. You will know your own circumstances best, but we recommend you be absent for a good portion of the advisory committee meeting. Ideas will surface and discussion might flow better. In addition, fringe ideas will emerge. These are ideas that would not come up with you present because people might think they were too obvious or so unsophisticated or outrageous they would not meet with your approval.

Your help is necessary at the outset of the meeting to get the discussion under way and to respond to questions. But be cautious about offering too much guidance or direction; you do not want to inhibit the spontaneity of the discussion. Then excuse yourself. Explain that you want to give the group the greatest latitude possible and that you hope to hear some outrageous suggestions. That way you will know you have tapped the full extent of the group's potential.

The second type of advisory committee is composed of members of groups in the community that you expect to be interested in your seminar. It is usually easy to get their cooperation. This surprises some people, but you have only to ask people you encounter during the day their opinions on subjects discussed in the newspaper to find that most of them are more than eager to tell you what they think. The same goes for opinions solicited by professionals in the community. If, for example you intend to offer a seminar you hope will appeal to special education teachers and administrators, a phone call to the Directors of Special Education in several local school districts will yield an enthusiastic committee. One reason for this cooperation is that many professional practitioners, physicians, teachers, attorneys, psychologists, social workers, nurses, speech pathologists, and school administrators (among others, of course) believe that outsiders do not understand them or their work. They are often frustrated in efforts to obtain support from those outside their profession. So when you let people know you want their advice for a program you are planning, you will find eager volunteers. Be specific about the issues to be discussed and what you want them to do. This is a subtle business because you want them to address your agenda, but at the same time you do not want to close down their thinking in a way that would deny you the opportunity to learn about topics or interests that you might not have been able to guide them to yourself.

For example, we conducted a long series of very successful 1-, 2-, and 3-day seminars and workshops for special education teachers, psychologists, social workers, and school administrators on Attention-Deficit/Hyperactivity Disorder (AD/HD). We wanted to develop selected aspects of these programs that could be angled for other audiences but still remain within the educational setting. We set up several advisory groups to help us. We explained our needs and asked them to respond to questions, such as

- What is the greatest need among educators for programs of this sort?
- Who else in the educational community needs help understanding AD/HD?
- What is the best way to reach them?
- What sort of advertising will stimulate their interest and encourage them to attend?

What we found in the discussion, however, was, no matter what we did to hold the topic to a discussion of Attention-Deficit/Hyperactivity Disorder, the conversation always kept turning to the more generic issue of behavior and discipline problems. The conversation might include behavior problems caused by AD/HD, but it also went considerably beyond the specifics of this one disorder.

This experience led to the development of our seminar "Practical Discipline Strategies for Classroom Teachers." It is unlikely we would have thought of this topic on our own. It was not that we were ignorant of the issue or that it was so far removed from several other seminars, including the AD/HD program we were already doing. Rather, it would not have occurred to us because our experience led us to our seminar topics from a different direction. Our specialized knowledge got in our way. Because of our training and professional orientation, we thought in terms of diagnoses, or specific identified problems, such as AD/HD or Conduct Disorder (CD) or Oppositional Defiant Disorder (ODD). We knew that children with a variety of these problems (and we were prepared to do programs on all of them) presented as discipline problems, but it took teachers who worked every day to tell us how they conceptualized their problems. They did not think in terms of diagnoses or the labels we used. They had their own labels to define their experience. It matters little to a teacher in the classroom whether a child's defiance reflects AD/HD, ODD, CD, or any other problem; it all looks the same to the teacher - a discipline problem.

We found we were able to attract a different audience to our programs on "Practical Discipline Strategies." While the AD/HD program appealed mainly to special education teachers and those who were already familiar with the diagnosis, such as school psychologists and social workers, a larger number of regular education teachers and administrators were attracted to the program on discipline because we were talking their language and addressing a problem as it existed in their minds. No amount of careful planning or brainstorming that excludes the targeted audience will give you the rich and stimulating mixture of ideas that you get with a group of people actually involved on a day-to-day basis with the problem.

Who would you like to comprise your audience? This will require a little thought. You may choose a broad definition, but you are better off if you can narrow it down. "Secretaries in small professional offices" is better than "secretaries in business offices," which is better than "secretaries." "Experienced secretaries in small business offices" is better yet. "Nurses in private medical offices" is better than "nurses," but "nurses in private pediatric offices" is better still. "Special education teachers" is better than "teachers." "Elementary special education teachers" is still better, and "elementary special education teachers with 1 to 2 years experience" is even better.

The advantage of a tight focus on whom you will survey, and ultimately sell your seminars, should be obvious. The better you focus on topics that will appeal to the audience, the better you will develop an efficient and less expensive advertising system. There is a disadvantage inherent in too much attention to a tightly defined population or too narrow a focus on a target audience, too.

You may define the audience so narrowly that you not only limit your potential registrants but miss many people on the fringes of your defined group who might have an interest.

Stay alert to the comments you hear from the critic in your own mind, the critic that insists you cannot proceed until every small detail of definition of your audience is complete. There is a subtle danger in investing too much time in defining your market. Too much concern about who the market is or too much effort given to defining it and focusing your topic, if done at an early stage of program development, can serve as a barrier to getting started. In the final analysis, the best design strategies and marketing ideas often grow out of real life experiences. Do not allow excessive planning to serve as an excuse for actually getting started. For example, we spent a lot of time planning and developing an outline for this book. We read books on related topics, examined material from dozens of seminars, and refined the outline and content guide. But we could have done that forever and never had an absolutely perfect design. It's the same with you. At some point you have to get started writing or designing or presenting.

FOCUS GROUPS

A focus group is a specialized advisory group. It may provide you with information an advisory group cannot. A focus group usually consists of 8 or 10 individuals who resemble people you hope to attract to your seminar. The task of the focus group is to respond to ideas and material already developed. This may include the title of your seminar or the program itself. We use focus groups to examine early drafts of all our promotional material to make sure we are on the right track. By asking this tightly constructed group to respond to what we already have in mind, we get a good idea of what works and what does not. They are right there in front of us to explain why something may or may not work, and they are able to offer ideas about what would work better.

For example, we usually have a focus group read our flyers and brochures. We ask for general responses such as whether it appeals to their eye and if they would be likely to read past the first line or two, but then we also ask questions about what they think the program is about. What does this flyer tell you this program will cover? What benefits will the person who attends gain? What sort of person does this flyer appeal to? The overriding questions are what is working the way you expect it to and what is not. If it doesn't work, why not? What can you do to fix it so it has the desired result? A single meeting with a focus group will delight you as you see how quickly you can obtain information that fine tunes your printed material and seminar into a salable product.

Of course, you have to approach this exercise with an open mind. Some of the lines you wrote for your brochure and some of the examples you want to use in your seminar, the ones you like most, the ones that you really love, are going to turn out to be some of the ones that do not work. You are the expert; run all the advice you get past your own critical eye, but remember your focus group can do something you cannot: They can look at you and your material the way your potential audience will, and that feedback is invaluable.

Remember that we want the focus group to tell us more than what worked or what did not. We want to learn why it did not work or why it did not have the intended impact. If the message is obscure, we want to find out what we have to alter to make it clear. Even if everything is clear, it may not mean the same to your focus group as it meant to you. On and on we go with focus groups until they have helped define precisely what is to be said. Finally, they will certify with their approval and understanding the best way to write or say it. Now you are ready to approach your wider audience.

SURVEYS AND QUESTIONNAIRES

Surveys are helpful, inexpensive, and easy to use. You can employ surveys with different audiences or potential audiences and thus get information about the breadth of interest in your topic and discover additional ideas or angles you might adapt to fit into niches you had not thought about before.

Whom Should You Ask?

Facing the prospect of survey research, many professionals who are comfortable and confident in their offices or clinics stop abruptly and cannot think of where to begin with a survey or questionnaire. Keep in mind that not all surveys utilize questionnaires. Just asking the next five people you meet a question or two is a survey. There are places for sophisticated and expensive surveys covering topics in depth and breadth, but in our own work we always start small. Modest surveys usually provide the information we need. If necessary, surveys can be expanded or refined. We usually get all the information we need to develop a seminar with only a modest investment of time and a few dollars.

National, State, and Local
Professional Organizations

We said surveys need not involve questionnaires. You don't even have to ask people questions to do some surveys. You can conduct an informal survey by asking professional organizations to put you on their mailing list to receive the annual national and state convention programs. You will also receive notices of local community lecture series, special seminars, and programs offered to members throughout the year. In similar fashion you can spend some time in the library studying what programs are offered by these professional organizations, and this will lead to ideas you can use and refine. Don't limit yourself to your own profession when you are looking for topics. If you are a psychologist, see what is of current concern to psychiatrists and social workers, too. If you are a psychiatrist, see what psychiatric nurses, psychologists, social workers, and marriage and family counselors are reading and studying. If you are a pediatric nurse, see what OB-GYN nurses, school nurses, home health care providers, and others are doing. If you work with children, remember that school social workers, counselors, and school psychologists all have journals, newsletters, national conferences, and local meetings with subjects that might be useful to you. Look at them all.

You can contact a few people you know in different occupations and ask them to pass along to you all the flyers, brochures, and other solicitations for seminars and short courses they receive over a 3-month period. These will give you some idea of your competition. They may or may not have been developed with good market research, so they are best viewed as stimuli for your own creative thinking, not something to be copied. Keep a record. Don't rely on your memory. A simple grid or chart that lists topics and intended audience will suffice. Write down the full title and any other information that gives you clues about the angle placed on the topic. You will be interested to see not just how many programs are offered on, say, adjustment to divorce, or being the spouse of an alcoholic, or caring for older parents but also the angles or emphasis placed on the topic. Be equally attentive to the intended audience. There is quite a bit of difference between a talk on caring for elderly parents given to adult children and a program for the therapists who will counsel adult children. As a bonus, by the time you complete your survey of other seminar offerings, you will have a substantial amount of data on practical matters, such as pricing, brochure styles, other advertising methods, and places to hold meetings.

Informal Telephone Surveys

An informal survey by telephone is the easiest and cheapest way to get good information. If you call a clinic, hospital, agency, or private office, you will have to explain who you are, what you want to know, and with whom you want to speak. If you do not have anyone's name, explain the nature of the job or position of the person you want to talk to. When starting out, you may not know who is the best source of information. It may be the office manager, the clinical director, the chief psychologist, the head of nursing or social work, or one of the physicians or therapists on the staff. Arrange for a convenient time to call back for the interview. This will involve a little recordkeeping to make sure you follow up at the proper time. It will also cause some frustration as you find that, even when you follow up promptly, there is not always someone available to talk to you. But most people are eager to help, and if you run into one office where the person you want to talk to is busy or not inclined to cooperate, you will find another who will help. Be prepared to ask straightforward questions using the questionnaire we will discuss later in this chapter as a guide. But leave some time for open-ended questions, too, just as we suggest in printed questionnaires.

You may be able to accomplish as much with an approach even less formal. Call a half-dozen nurses or physical therapists or pediatricians or psychologists or anyone else you want to interview and talk to whomever you can reach at that time. You will be pleased at how much information you can get from only a small number of interviews. It might be enough to get you started on your seminar design. Brief survey methods are most helpful if you are at work in an area where you already have a good deal of knowledge. If you are expanding into territory where you are learning the content at the same time you are searching for marketable ideas, you will need much more from your informants.

Using Your Advisory Committee

Enlist the help of your advisory committee. Members may work in a clinic, school, or hospital where they can speak with a number of people, or they may be able to suggest names for follow-up phone calls. They may also be able to arrange to have your questionnaire printed and distributed to coworkers. Advisors may belong to community groups or professional organizations that will give you further access to people to survey. Be alert for opportunities for greater efficiency, such as using your advisory committee as more than just a source of ideas. It is usually difficult to plan this synergy, but if you remain alert, you will find ways to use limited resources to yield maximum gain. For example, a nurse from the local hospital who serves on one of our advisory committees has distributed survey questionnaires throughout his hospital. He also collects and returns them. When it is time to advertise a program he takes a supply of brochures and distributes them to hospital staff using their internal mail system, saving a lot of postage.

In a similar way, professional or community organizations will, under certain circumstances, include your surveys with their regular mailing. We have used this technique quite a bit. It costs very little - often no more than a share of the overall mailing cost or a contribution to the organization. It is to your advantage, of course, if someone from the organization is on your advisory committee and can vouch for the quality and professionalism of your work and, most importantly, its relevance and value to the members of the organization. This same distribution channel will then be available for your brochures or other promotional material.

Questionnaires

We use questionnaires for three main purposes:

1. To develop a list of topics of interest to target audiences.
2. To obtain information about the needs the audience has regarding the topics.
3. Marketing. Remember, anything you do to put your name in front of someone is marketing - even if it is a questionnaire asking for help and telling them you are planning to offer a service in the future.

If this is your initial questionnaire, you will want to ask four questions:

1. What topics would be most helpful to you in a seminar?
2. If we could cover only one of them, which one would it be?
3. What problems encountered in your daily work might this seminar help with?
4. Under what circumstances are you most likely to attend?

The first two questions provide topics and subtopics. We use a modular design for our seminars. This simply means we develop a number of relatively self-contained segments that address specific subtopics and put them together into a full-sized seminar. There must be good overall organization, of course, but with a modular design you can string specific topics together like a strand of pearls, each with its own value, but, when taken together, they form an object of even greater beauty.

The modular design has additional advantages. It enables you to shift the emphasis or organization of the seminar to respond to different audiences or varying needs or time frames. It also makes it easier to fit your material to other media, such as audiotape or videotape. We will have more to say about modular design in Chapter 3.

The third question is designed to open up discussion of the perceived needs of the individual answering your questionnaire. A person can usually list many topics that might be interesting, but none of them might touch on strongly felt needs. These needs may seem obvious from the topics suggested. The head of nursing in a hospital may want more information on AIDS for her staff nurses since more people are asking nurses questions that go unanswered. The supervisor assumes this is because nurses need to know more facts. But if you survey the staff nurses, you may find that the "communication problem" has nothing to do with lack of information. Rather, many nurses avoid discussing AIDS among themselves or with patients because they are frightened. While they acknowledge the seriousness of the topic, they deny the immediacy and relevance to their own work in order to distance themselves from the threat of the disease. So, even if you come in and give them the best lecture in the world, they may not be able to use what you give them if the issue of their feelings and fears are not addressed.

The fourth question inquires into which day of the week is best, what time of the day people are most likely to attend, whether there are times or days when they would never attend, and whether who is paying for the program - themselves or their employer - will have a substantial effect on their decision to attend. This latter point might seem obvious. After all, wouldn't everyone be more likely to attend if someone else paid for registration? To some extent, this is likely to be a useful generalization but may not be relevant to your particular program.

The target audience for one of our programs on Attention-Deficit/Hyperactivity Disorder is educators. But we market the same program to parents of children who have AD/HD as well. Many teachers and school administrators attend the program even if they have to pay out of their own pockets, but, of course, many more attend only if their school will foot the bill.

It is not the same for parents. If they have the interest and if they can afford the registration fee, they will attend. Therefore, the determining factor for parents is the cost. Take this issue into account.

The general form of the questionnaire we use when we are developing new topics for seminars is presented on pages 45-47. This sample questionnaire focuses on the needs and interests of nurses; however, it could easily be adapted to any other professional or lay group.

The questionnaire and advisory group can work together. The advisory group will find the results of your questionnaire interesting, and this will stimulate further discussion. They will be able to use the results of the survey to expand on their own ideas and gain some idea of where their ideas fit in with those of the people you surveyed, and it will also give you some idea of the reliability and validity of the survey results if they make sense to your advisory committee.

Sending questionnaires by mail can be expensive. And when you get them back, collating and interpreting the data can be a daunting task. But there are small steps and shortcuts to consider before embarking on a major survey project. How many questionnaires do you need? The answer depends on what you want to do with the results. If the purpose of your questionnaire is to prepare a formal research report, there are statistical guidelines that will let you know what sort of numbers you need to be sure your statistics are meaningful. But that is not why we use questionnaires in the seminar business. We use them to get ideas and one good idea can come from one questionnaire from one person. We use questionnaires in a sequential process.

If you distribute 20 questionnaires and the responses are fairly consistent, the reliability of the data will encourage you to act on it. But what will you make of 20 questionnaires that yield entirely different answers? How will you make sense of them? This may result from a sample size that was too small, but, more likely, you did not formulate your questions with sufficient care. The responses you received varied widely because your questions were too vague, subject to individual interpretation, or just hard to understand. Examine the results and fine-tune your questionnaire. Send it to another 20 people. You will learn more about people's thoughts about your topic.

Try to keep the questionnaire to a single sheet of paper. The questions should be answerable by making check marks or circling items with a few questions that are open ended so you do not close off the opportunity to get information you may not have considered on your own.

Let's say you begin by preparing a one-page questionnaire (both sides of the sheet of paper is okay), and you want 20 responses. You can mail a survey of this type first-class for $12.80 including return postage - excluding, of course, the cost of your time spent on the project. If you prefer 10 times as many questionnaires, it will be to your advantage to look for a cheaper way to distribute them. For example, if the questionnaire will be distributed to a group of secretaries in one company, nurses in one hospital or office, physicians in one practice, or attorneys in one group, the questionnaires can be marked with individual names and put in a large envelope and mailed parcel post to the office building, hospital, or clinic with a note inside asking that the items be distributed. You can promise to stop by and pick them up or send individual stamped return envelopes. If there are only a few locations but a lot of people, you can hand deliver the packages. Variations of this idea depend on what your relationship is with the group you are surveying, whether you have their cooperation, or whether you are doing a cold survey. This will also influence how many people respond. (We will return to this idea of how to distribute material at lowest cost when we discuss marketing your program.) You should always be on the lookout for alternative distribution systems for your questionnaires or promotional materials that avoid the heavy costs of mail or traditional advertising.

Once you have analyzed the questionnaire results, make lists of tentative topics. At this stage topics should be fairly broad.

Think of them as the titles of half- or 1-day programs. Now it may be helpful to do one more questionnaire survey. List the topics and ask another group of 20 people to respond to a similar questionnaire. (See Sample Follow-Up Questionnaire on pp. 49-50.)

Start With Your Own Strength

Some experts advise that the place to begin a seminar project is to identify your target audience before you begin to think about a topic for your program. For example, Howard Shenson, author of *How to Develop & Promote Successful Seminars & Workshops* (1990), claims this assessment should take precedence even for those who may hope to rely on their own specialized knowledge or professional information.

"Starting out with a market orientation," says Shenson, "spares them from wasting time and money becoming hapless inventors. Rather than dreaming up topics that seem like good ideas, but that no one really needs or wants, successful promoters tailor their ideas to fit a clearly identifiable market or market segment. When the topic finally selected for presentation at the seminar is of sufficient interest to this market, a profitable outcome for the promoters is insured" (pp. 1-2).

Like any generalization, Shenson's comments are worth considering - up to a point. We agree it is important, even vital, to keep your market in mind at all times. But in practice, we usually use a combination of market assessment and an appraisal of our own interests and skills with an emphasis on what we know we can do best as the dominant factor at the outset of planning.

There is an old adage in the seminar business: Choose topics you either know a great deal about or topics you feel passionate about. You would not want to put a great deal of effort into the development of any topic until you give careful thought to your market, but to start with only market considerations may deny you the very topics that you will be able to infuse with the greatest enthusiasm.

In our experience, problems arise if you start only with the market assessment, just as there can be problems if you start only with your own interests. How do you assess your market? How do you choose the market? How do you fit what you know best to the target market? You could be in the position of having to alter that which you know best or dilute or reframe it in a way that takes away the special spark that can only add to the topic. So don't be afraid of the possible problems. Many of them will test you in ways that will open your eyes to new opportunities. There is more to the seminar business than just simple common sense, but that does not mean you should ever abandon that common sense.

ANGLES AND NICHES

Angles

Every seminar has an angle, that is, a point of view or emphasis. You will have to decide how to angle your seminar and then think about what marketing niches to address. Suggesting that we look for a marketing angle may cause hesitation. In common parlance, looking for an angle often means looking for an unfair advantage or suggests a sharp business practice. That's not the kind of angle we are talking about. Writers use the word "angle" as a synonym for the slant or emphasis given to a story. The same topic may interest different groups for different reasons, so depending on your audience, you may organize the program around different aspects of the topic.

For example, you may have tremendous knowledge of green beans because of your interest in gardening. So you write an article for the magazine *Today's Gardener* on "Varieties of Beans and the Best Fertilizer to Help Them Grow." But your knowledge of beans is so extensive that you don't stop there. You prepare another article for *American History* magazine on the extensive use of beans as a source of protein in victory gardens during World War II. You title your piece "Beans Go to War: Use of Six Varieties of Beans to Provide Protein for the Folks at Home During World War II." But your creativity is still not exhausted, so you write, from a slightly different angle but still about beans, an article for *Modern Nutrition* titled "Beans, the All-Around Vegetable."

And you are still not finished. You follow that article with a novel piece for the magazine *Decorating Tips and Ideas* titled "How to use Dried Bean Stalks to Weave Colorful Placements." Now that is finding the slants and angles in your topic.

Drug Awareness Recognition Education (DARE) police officers and others involved with drug prevention programs provide another example of angling a topic. They are attracted to our programs on Attention-Deficit/Hyperactivity Disorder because children with AD/HD are at higher risk for alcohol and other drug problems as adolescents and young adults. Effective treatment reduces that risk. That's the angle we use to promote AD/HD programs to these groups. The angle we have used to sell the AD/HD program to groups of teachers and parents of learning disabled (LD) children has multiple foci. We stress that it is often difficult to tell AD/HD from LD, and about 35% to 40% of children in school programs for the learning disabled have AD/HD but were never diagnosed. Every parent and educator of children with learning disabilities should be alert to AD/HD. The second point is that AD/HD and LD often overlap, and teaching children with LD can be much more effective if people understand the AD/HD, too.

The core of the programs we offer learning disability educators or DARE officers is not different than what we offer others, but there is a change in the amount of time we spend on differentiating AD/HD from LD or on drug-related issues, and we may change the order of the topics to make issues clearer. We do the same angling when we write articles for different magazines or journals. An article on AD/HD in a medical journal for pediatricians may contain a lot of the same material as an article in the journal of the National Association of School Psychologists, but it is likely that different issues will be emphasized.

You may be especially knowledgeable about anxiety disorders. Angles include diagnosis of anxiety disorders, current research on the biological causes of anxiety disorders, psychotherapy of anxiety, and pharmacotherapy of anxiety. Each of these topics might be expected to attract a different audience. There would certainly be overlap; many nonmedical psychologists may be interested in the biology of anxiety as well as treatment with medication, but those topics would most likely appeal to physicians. Use of psychological tests to diagnose anxiety disorders would appeal more to psychologists, but any topic on diagnosis might be expected to attract psychologists, psychiatrists, clinical social workers, and possibly lay members of the community.

But there are other angles that might attract different audiences. For example, you could offer a program on reactive or transient anxiety associated with divorce. Or present programs on loss in general, but subdivide the topic with angles that focus on loss in divorce, death of an elderly spouse, death of a child, chronic illness of a child or spouse, or death of a parent. You should be able to sit with a notepad and pen and list a number of different angles for your primary topic. Eventually, if you draw a few connecting lines you will have sketched a branching tree. Broad or general ideas will form the main branches; specific or narrow topics will create smaller branches. This will suggest even more angles. As you work up the different angles, you will think of even more. Your reading will be affected, and you will notice things you may have missed in the past. You will see the angles that are suggested in your topic, but also you will see how journal, newspaper, and magazine writers have taken often familiar topics and given them an angle or slant. Not every angle is a separate program or seminar. Some are too narrow. Some are best grouped with others because they are not substantial enough to stand on their own. Some are interesting, but it is not likely you will find an audience of sufficient size to make them worth developing further. Some will be trivial or contrived.

Niches

Finding market niches differs from angling the topic. The same angle may appeal to people who occupy different niches. For example, federal guidelines issued by the Agency for Health Care Policy and Research, an arm of the Department of Health and Human Services, claim that stroke victims recover better if they are assessed for depression and placed in rehabilitation programs that fit their needs. About 550,000 Americans suffer

strokes each year, and most survive. There are many angles suggested by this recommendation, including informing primary care
and specialty physicians and all the other professionals who work
with stroke victims. There are angles on training physicians and
other mental health care workers to assess and treat these patients.

But where are all the professionals and laymen and laywomen
who might be interested in these programs? They are clustered in
different niches, some of which are obvious, but some of which
are not. Is there a niche at the annual meeting of nurses who
provide gerontological care? At their state meeting? Their local
meeting? Where will we find the families of stroke victims?
They certainly will be a good audience for a program on how
strokes cause depression and the effect this can have on the patient's family. What about rehabilitation centers? Where do
stroke victims go for rehabilitation or convalescent care? Who are
the professionals besides physicians and nurses who care for them?
Who else besides physical therapists (PTs) and occupational therapists (OTs)? Where will you find the PT and OT audiences? Do
they hold annual meetings? Who else might be interested in the
rehabilitation of stroke victims and represent niches for your
programs? How about the private rehabilitation company that has
a contract with the stroke victim's insurance company and is eager
to do whatever can be done to return the younger stroke patient to
gainful employment as soon as possible? Certainly they will want
to know about psychological features of their clients that might
have an impact on rehabilitation efforts.

These are niches. Niche implies a small place, and many are
small in the sense that they are not obvious in the way a school
district, large general hospital, or factory is obvious, but niches
need not be small. A focus on niches is useful because it forces
you to think about who might be interested in what you have to
offer. Finally, there is more to identifying a niche than just finding another market segment to flood with brochures. Once we
have identified a niche, we want to own it. We market heavily to
people in the niche: locally, across the state, or across the country. We want to be major players in that niche. We want to have
our reputation spread, and we try to build it in a cost-effective
way.

Niches are not just places where you might find people interested in your topic. They are defined segments of the market that can be reached with a targeted marketing strategy. For example, here are some niches we identified for our program on Attention-Deficit/Hyperactivity Disorder: Special education teachers, school nurses, pediatric office nurses, school teacher aides, high school counselors, DARE officers, other drug prevention programs, adoption workers, Aid to Families with Dependent Children (AFDC) caseworkers, parents of children with learning disabilities, police youth officers, juvenile court staff, alternative school programs, and educators of the deaf.

The way we discovered the niche of deaf educators is instructive. We had presented our general program on AD/HD in several cities and a half-dozen times had inquiries from state schools for the deaf as well as public school programs for the deaf asking if we could tailor some of our remarks for them. They had particular problems with children with AD/HD because they could often not distinguish problems related to hearing loss from symptoms that might be indicative of attention problems. This set us on a new track and led to consideration of close captioning our videotapes for educators of the deaf and the deaf themselves. It also taught us that the interest a group may have in a topic does not depend on sheer numbers. After all, how many deaf children with AD/HD are there in a particular school district or even in one state school for the deaf? But these children, no matter how rare, present a considerable challenge for their teachers. The teachers (and the students) have a strong need for information in this area. Here again we see the issue of need develop. Need for help does not depend on the number of these children in this case but on how much of a perceived need it is from the people involved.

We are a small company with a limited range of services to sell. We compete every day with large companies that do the same work we do. For example, several publishers of major textbooks on AD/HD have national seminar programs that they market with a lot more financial clout than we can manage. But their size is also a source of their vulnerability. They cannot easily identify and adapt to the niche marketing we do. We solicit the same large potential audience they do, but we go them one better and add the niches, too.

Fads Versus Topics of Sustained Interest

We view seminars as dynamic entities. They change constantly. Therefore, even if you develop only one program and meet with such success that you continue to offer your program over several years, your program will evolve and change, often without conscious effort or decision on your part.

Your presentation will be modified by the feedback you get. The content will be altered by new things you learn. The structure will shift in different ways as you become more comfortable and familiar with the material. Examples and illustrations will change or be added as you encounter experiences that can be incorporated into the program. Your creation develops and grows richer and more complex. It feels terrific. It is the same with any creative endeavor that grows richer as time passes. And you will encounter suggestions and experiences that suggest new avenues of approach, angles on your topic, and other marketing niches where there might be interest in what you have to present. In fact, you are likely to find that you will want to spin off a portion of your program or expand the seminar in some way.

You may find that your workshop touches on a topic that is in the spotlight for a short time. For example, as part of our program on Attention-Deficit/Hyperactivity Disorder, we discuss fad treatments that have no scientific validity, such as diet and vitamin and mineral supplements. That represents only 15 to 20 minutes of a day-long program. But several years ago there was an upsurge of interest in the popular press about allergies and food sensitivities and the effect on behavior and learning in children in general. There were a number of articles that appeared in popular magazines about cytologic testing, whose advocates argued that they could tell whether a child had an allergy, food sensitivity, or chemical imbalance by testing saliva or a few strands of hair. Because children with AD/HD often have associated learning or behavioral problems, their parents and teachers were very interested in these reports.

None of this had any scientific validity, however. Because of our work with children with AD/HD, we were knowledgeable about the role of food sensitivity and allergies and their relationships to AD/HD symptoms, but we were not experts. So we went to the experts at the medical center in our community and to the scientific literature. Then, rather than offer this information as a program of our own, we contacted several good-sized outpatient mental health clinics and offered the program to them as a practice builder. We were not sure that the market would support a seminar of this type to the extent that we could make it profitable. It is certainly possible that it could have been a very good program for us, but at the time we thought it would be most efficient to look for an alternative way to deliver the program.

One of the clinics decided to use the program with the lengthy title "Can You Really Help Your Child Deal With a Learning Problem or Attention-Deficit/Hyperactivity Disorder or Behavioral Difficulty by Change of Diet or Giving Vitamins?" They offered the program at no charge as part of their community service and practice building effort. We helped them organize it and were available to present part of the program if they wanted us to, but they had knowledgeable staff available, so we collected our consulting fee for developing and organizing the program and left the rest to them.

In essence, this was a response to a fad, but, we think, a good response. There is still residual interest in dietary treatment of a variety of behavior and learning disorders, and several authors of well-known books continue to appear on talk shows promoting their ideas, but the large interest has died down. We probably would not get as good a response to this topic today from either the mental health clinics or the public.

There are good responses and bad responses to fads. The good ones are those based on careful evaluation of the circumstances and an assessment of how your involvement in this topic might serve the goals you have set for yourself. After that the decision to follow or abandon the fad is not difficult.

But at first you will want to choose your best topic, one that you can organize and present best and one that is most likely to appeal to the largest audience. Also choose a topic that will have sustained interest so you can come back to it again and again not only to reap the immediate rewards but also to gain experience and practice. This will allow you to work with the topic long enough to refine it as well as learn the seminar business by actually doing it. Later topics and applications of some of the finer points in this book will be easier with a solid chunk of experience in your pocket.

What About All the Competition Out There?

Well, what about it? There are a lot of people and organizations presenting seminars, lectures, courses, and workshops on just about every topic they can think of. If you are hesitant and unsure of yourself, you might be intimidated and tempted toward self-doubt. Can you find anything to add to the furious conversations already taking place that will encourage people to register for your seminar? On the other hand, if you have enough confidence in yourself, you might view the same environment and say, "Wow! There must be a heck of a market out there for seminars if there are so many already being offered. Surely, there is room for one more first class offering."

Of course, there's room for one more. And one more after that, and still another. Actually, the abundance of seminars, workshops, courses, conferences, and other programs is a testimony to the vast interest that exists and the relative ease with which it is possible to join the game - as long as you do a good job with the fundamentals. Define your audience, assess their needs, and define your niche. Finally, put together a good marketing program. Success will follow.

Don't be afraid to be wrong. If you wait until you are absolutely sure your idea is going to be a success, you will never start. If you wait until your design or marketing plans are certain to be correct, you will never get started. We have worked in this business long enough to recognize in ourselves, and the others with whom we consult, that extended debate over color of a brochure, extensive searches to be certain we are not missing some small segment of a market known to an obscure mailing list broker, or even debate about whether to alter some element of the design of the seminar itself are not instances of careful and responsible planning but stalling tactics. Listen to the experts, of course, but you are the most expert in your topic area. Trust your own judgment most of all.

Exercise for Selecting Topics

Think about yourself personally and professionally and answer the following questions with the first response that occurs to you. Fill in every line even if you have to struggle.

1. People tell me I know a lot about

    a. _____
    b. _____
    c. _____
    d. _____
    e. _____

2. When I get "wound up" I really go on and on about

    a. _____
    b. _____
    c. _____
    d. _____
    e. _____

3. I think people need to know a lot more about

    a. _____
    b. _____
    c. _____
    d. _____
    e. _____

4.   There sure seems to be a lot of ignorance about

   a. _____

   b. _____

   c. _____

   d. _____

   e. _____

5.   Boy, if someone gave me an audience, I'd just love to talk about

   a. _____

   b. _____

   c. _____

   d. _____

   e. _____

Sample Questionnaire

We are preparing a series of lectures, seminars, and workshops for nurses and would like your ideas and opinions about programs that would have the most practical value. These seminars will be presented by experienced nurses, but even the best programs have to reflect the practical needs of people on the job. Thank you for your help.

1. What are three topics you would like to see as part of a 1-day continuing education program? (Please put a check mark next to the one you view as most important.)

    a. _____

    b. _____

    c. _____

2. Please tell us any specific needs you have in regard to these topics. What do you need to aid you in your practice?

    a. _____

    b. _____

    c. _____

3. What program would you be most likely to attend?

    _____

    _____

    _____

    _____

4. In your experience, what topics for continuing education do you think nurses new to the profession need most?

    a. _____

    b. _____

    c. _____

5. Does your hospital/office have a formal program of continuing education for nurses?

    ☐ Yes   ☐ No

6. Does your employer offer financial support for you to attend continuing education programs offered by organizations outside your place of employment?

    ☐ Yes   ☐ No

7. On what day would you be most likely to attend a full-day program that interested you?

    ☐ Monday   ☐ Saturday
    ☐ Tuesday   ☐ Sunday
    ☐ Wednesday   ☐ Any day as long as it was
    ☐ Thursday   my day off
    ☐ Friday

8. Is there a day you would never attend a program even if it held high interest for you?

    ☐ Yes   ☐ No

    If yes, which day(s)? _____

9. What time of day would you prefer to attend a half-day (about 3½ hours) program?

    ☐ Morning   ☐ Afternoon   ☐ Evening

10. Is there a time of day you would never attend such a program?

    ☐ Yes   ☐ No

    If yes, when? _____

Continuing education programs are often offered by people who are not working with patients on a day-to-day basis and do not have the insight full-time practitioners do about what it is that nurses really need. Is there anything else you can tell us about your needs that will help us design programs that are more useful for you?

_____

_____

_____

_____

_____

_____

_____

Sample Follow-Up Questionnaire

Listed below are six topics we are planning to offer as seminars. Please circle the number that indicates the extent of your interest in each of these topics. Thank you.

A. New medical and psychological treatment techniques for headaches

   1......2.......3.......4.......5......6.......7......8......9........10
   Not   Somewhat   Very
   Interested   Interested   Interested

B. Raising a responsible self-confident child

   1......2.......3.......4.......5......6.......7......8......9........10
   Not   Somewhat   Very
   Interested   Interested   Interested

C. Creative renewal: Stress management for teachers

   1......2.......3.......4.......5......6.......7......8......9........10
   Not   Somewhat   Very
   Interested   Interested   Interested

D. Helping an aging parent

   1......2.......3.......4.......5......6.......7......8......9........10
   Not   Somewhat   Very
   Interested   Interested   Interested

E. Coordinating the care of patients with Alzheimer's disease

1......2......3......4......5......6......7......8......9........10
Not   Somewhat   Very
Interested   Interested   Interested

F. Nursing the patient with a closed-head injury

1......2......3......4......5......6......7......8......9........10
Not   Somewhat   Very
Interested   Interested   Interested

Please rank the three topics that interest you most.

Topic that interests me most (A-F): _____

Second most interesting topic (A-F): _____

Third most interesting topic (A-F): _____

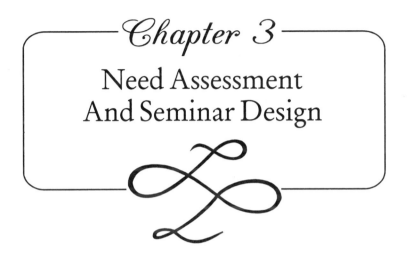

Chapter 3

Need Assessment
And Seminar Design

Designing an effective seminar requires careful planning. No doubt you can think of seminars you attended that were exciting learning experiences and others that were boring, uncomfortable events that seemed to last forever. To a great extent, the qualitative difference between these extremes results from how carefully the seminars were designed. Interesting material, excellent presentation skills, and wonderful facilities are essential, but not enough to create a first-rate seminar; you need a good design. And, because a good design involves a great deal of creativity, design can be fun.

A good seminar design is based on understanding how adults learn and follow a specific sequence of steps:

- Conduct a need assessment
- Write educational objectives
- Determine content areas/modules
- Design each module and form them into a cohesive program
- Deliver the seminar
- Evaluate the effectiveness of the seminar

NEED ASSESSMENT

Perceived Versus Actual Needs

The first step in developing an effective seminar is need assessment. We touched on this in Chapter 2 when we discussed market research to determine whether a potential seminar topic was viable. Therefore, if you have done even preliminary market research, you have already determined that some people perceive a need for your program. Need assessment now, however, extends these initial inquiries to determine what specific needs the audience has in regard to the topic you have chosen. Perceived needs, assessed during market research, are not always the same as actual needs. Do not be intimidated by the term "need assessment" or "need analysis." The seminar business, like any business has its own jargon. Need assessment just means we have to address our audience's needs, not what we think they need. And we have to distinguish what might interest them, or even what they might want, from what they need. You may want a new car, but if your present car runs well and finances are tight, it is unlikely anyone can sell you a new car. When you need one, when your current car is beyond repair, you will buy a new one.

A person can also need something and not want it. You may need treatment for alcoholism but not want it. Your supervisor may insist you need psychological treatment to learn to control your temper, but you may not want treatment or even perceive the need. On the other hand, you may want something and not need it. You may need additional training to interview a certain type of patient and not know it is needed, while other people may want additional training in, say, hypnosis because the idea appeals to them, but nothing in their practice requires hypnosis, or even if it does, the problems can be managed with the full range of other therapeutic modalities available.

A successful seminar will deliver what people need as well as what they think they need. Usually these needs are the same - but not always. The list of needs you establish will be developed further to become the behavioral objectives, which, in turn, will make clear what to put into your seminar and what to leave out.

Understanding people's needs allows the seminar presenter to build a program that meets those needs. Thus, there should be a benefit obtained from attending the seminar. The benefit fits the need. We place a strong emphasis on a careful determination of who your audience is and what needs you seek to fulfill. Few will register for your program unless they perceive a benefit to be gained. No people will walk away satisfied - even if you do a good job presenting the material - if they do not think they have received a benefit. This probably seems obvious, but it is the key to designing and marketing your program. You must meet the audience's needs, and you must provide a benefit. It is not enough to do a good job. It is not enough to be thorough in your presentation or discussion of a topic. Your audience must feel it has gained something from your presentation and most importantly you must have met its needs. We will have a lot more to say about this when we discuss marketing in Chapter 4, but for now we will stress that people buy a benefit. Your marketing has to strike the responsive chord that resonates to that perceived need. Their needs and the benefits they seek are not always clear, even to the participants in your program. Nonetheless the needs of your audience must always be a factor in your mind even from the earliest stages of program development. Let your development be guided by the question "What benefit does the audience want from this program?" and you will not go wrong.

Commitment to meeting the needs of your audience goes beyond holding yourself to the standard of thoroughness or an in-depth presentation. It is possible to present a program that might delight your colleagues and be a miserable failure for a different professional group or lay audience because, while all of them may have been interested in the topic, they had different needs. For example, as a psychologist you might offer a detailed discussion of the use of new psychological tests to differentiate antisocial personality disorder from depression and Attention-Deficit/Hyper-activity Disorder in adults. You explain in detail how to use the tests and satisfy all the psychologists in your audience because you met their need; they know the benefit they received: a new skill they can use. But what if your audience also includes clinical social workers or psychiatrists or others who have just as much interest in the differential diagnosis of these disorders and who were attracted by your announcement about new techniques to make these differentiations? They will certainly find a good portion of your presentation interesting, but you will not have met their needs or created the feeling in them of having received a substantial benefit. Their needs differ even if they are closely related to those of psychologists.

Determining the Audience's Needs

The obvious way to start gathering information about what your audience needs is to ask a representative group of people what their needs are. Certainly you'll want to do this and will probably include your advisory group in the list of folks you'll ask about these needs. If, for instance, your seminar is on "Effective Patient Communication in the General Medical Office," you will want to ask nurses and physicians, as well as technical and clerical staff, about problems they experience communicating with patients and what specific needs they have in this area. You'll no doubt get an earful because your market research has already determined a need for this general program. There will be different perceptions within an office depending on the nature of a person's job. Moreover, the perceptions of nurses asked to comment on how the clerical staff or physicians communicate may differ from what the clerical staff or what the physicians tell you based on their self-appraisal. Furthermore, each of these groups will have its own notions of problems and needs of the nursing staff. You will also want to ask your advisory group for help with their ideas about the needs of your intended audience.

It is important to distinguish between real needs and perceived needs. No matter how you ask the members of the medical office staff about their needs, all they can give you are their own *perceptions* of what they need. While their perceptions are important and probably accurate, the staff's perceptions are only one very simple form of a need assessment. Rarely can people be objective enough to really see what all their needs are. Let's suppose that questioning members of a medical office staff reveals problems in two areas: (a) patients' attention to and understanding of instructions for their medical care and (b) other family members' interference with treatment plans. But what if we asked patients what they felt the communication problems were? Do you think patients would say they did not listen well? If we interviewed family members, is it likely that they would say that they interfere with medical care? Probably not! Or, if we asked physicians about nurses' or nurses about physicians' communication problems, would both groups list the same needs? It is unlikely, even though these different perspectives are all valuable. Confusion and contradiction arise because we often don't know what we don't know.

Who Feels the Need?

The perception of need does not always arise in the person who will attend your seminar. Need also comes from perceptions of supervisors or employers. Employees' evaluations or restructured job descriptions may lead to needs. But keep in mind who your customer is. If a supervisor thinks there is a need to train workers but the employees do not feel the need, you will have to sell your seminar to the supervisor because you sure are not going to be able to sell it to the employees.

Another one of our own failures underscores this lesson. We were on a tour of several cities in Kentucky presenting seminars on school-related topics and chatting with teachers and school administrators about trends in education that might give us ideas for new programs. We learned that the State Superintendent of Education had just issued a directive to county superintendents requiring every school district to have an inclusion program. Inclusion refers to the practice of teaching students with special needs, such as learning disabilities or emotional problems, in regular, rather than separate special education, classrooms.

We couldn't wait to get back to our office to send a proposal to every school superintendent and principal in Kentucky offering a seminar/workshop designed to help regular education teachers manage the special learning and behavioral needs of all the special education students who would soon be crowding into their classrooms. We sent out the letters and proposals and waited for the response. But there was none. No one wrote and no one called.

Here is the lesson we learned. No one felt a need for our program. We had no benefit to sell. We later learned that many local superintendents who received the directive from the state office of education ordering inclusion ignored it. They were used to proclamations from central administrators and usually did not follow them. In counties and districts where inclusion programs were being implemented, no one felt a need for our programs either. Our timing was way off. Teachers and administrators had no experience with inclusion. They were not able to anticipate problems. If they could have predicted some of the problems they would face (and we could help solve), it was only at an intellectual level. Several years of frustration and failure trying to implement inclusion would still be necessary before educators would feel the need for a program such as ours.

In retrospect we can see why we did not hit the needs of these people. We knew classroom teachers would become frustrated with the demands made by the few children with special problems. We could anticipate their frustration because we had seen it so many times before. We can only guess what was going on in the teachers' minds at that time because we did not reach out to them for market research purposes or market the programs to them. We misdirected our marketing efforts to administrators.

The city and county superintendents to whom we wrote felt no need. Why should they? They had what they regarded as an excellent plan - on paper - to handle the whole program. The special education teachers they would free up by transferring their students to regular classrooms would be available as consultants to regular education teachers. The program would meet the philosophical needs of those who thought that all children should be taught in the same setting and would meet the budgetary needs of the school district because no additional staff or other expenses would be incurred. The plan would meet the needs of the teachers' union because no teachers would lose their jobs.

The simple fact that, in practice, this finely tuned plan was never going to work did not, at the time, matter. The men and women to whom we wanted to sell our consulting programs saw and felt absolutely no need, so no matter how forcefully we emphasized the strengths of our program and no matter how good they all agreed it looked, it met no need of theirs and consequently no one bought it. Finally, 3 years after some districts began to experiment with inclusion, we had the opportunity to approach them again at a time when frustration and their own experience led local administrators and their staffs to feel the need for some assistance in this area.

While a need assessment will determine what it is that members of your audience need, it is just as important to give full consideration to their perceived needs. They may be wrong about their needs or they may have an incomplete picture of their needs, but if you are not responsive to perceived needs, people who attend your seminar will leave with the feeling that you have not fully responded to what they regard as the most important part of their reason for attending.

Think for a minute about the nurses working in the medical office where there are communication problems. What if, when instructing patients on follow-up care, the majority used words that were too technical for their patients or violated a cultural expectation of these patients which caused a family member to "interfere." Would they necessarily be aware of either of these communication problems? Probably not, which is why it is essential to conduct a need assessment that includes other people in addition to your intended audience.

Need assessment addresses three subjects: (a) knowledge, (b) skills, and (c) attitudes/beliefs (about your topic area). These are the three possible areas in which to provide training. We begin with the question "What knowledge, skills, and attitudes or beliefs do we want members of the audience to possess?" Answering these questions will provide a picture of what we call the "exemplar" or model member of your intended audience. Our question for the staff of the medical office, on the subject of effective patient communications, is "What knowledge, skills, and attitudes/beliefs must they possess to be effective in communicating with patients and with each other?"

A list is drawn up for each area: knowledge, skills, and attitudes/beliefs. This will become what we will call a KSA chart.

The complete chart will provide a picture of the exemplar or ideal practitioner in the area of effective patient communication. The information needed to fill in these lists can, and should, come from a variety of sources. Chances are that you, having worked or practiced in the field for some time, will have a great many ideas of what to fill in. Go ahead. But then add to your list (or delete) by surveying other sources: your advisory committee, individuals representative of your intended audience, and other interested parties such as the patients, doctors, or supervisors. What knowledge, skills, and attitudes do these groups believe medical office staff must possess to be effective communicators with patients? We call this "full-view" a 360-degree assessment and is more valid than "self-report" from only intended audience members.

There are additional methods for obtaining information to complete this picture of the exemplar. Observation is an excellent way to see and hear the knowledge, skills, and attitudes of the exemplar. What is required is access to one or more people who have been identified as already acting as exemplars. This can be done by referral from knowledgeable sources or from more objective data, such as job ratings, which show this person to be an exemplar. Another method in creating a picture of the exemplar is to use documents, such as job descriptions, which tell what knowledge, skills, and attitudes are required of the exemplar in a given job.

Let's carry another example a little further. Assume that a therapist wants to offer a program on "Recognizing Eating Disorders in Students and Making Proper Referrals." The intended audience is primarily school personnel from middle and high schools, including teachers, counselors, nurses, and administrators. This therapist has specialized in eating disorders for 10 years, so she can fill in a good portion of the KSA chart herself. In addition, she has surveyed several colleagues to get their views on the characteristics of an exemplar teacher or counselor who could identify and refer students with eating disorders. Finally, she talked with three people from local schools who are representative of the intended audience who were identified by colleagues and supervisors as models for what all educators should be in the area

of eating disorders. The KSA chart developed is presented in
Table 3-1 (below).

TABLE 3-1: KNOWLEDGE-SKILLS-ATTITUDES/BELIEFS (KSA) CHART		
Knowledge	**Skills**	**Attitudes**
Forms of eating disorders (ED)	Use of referral sources	See as prevalent problem
Symptoms of each ED	Observation of ED behavior	Belief they have role
Causes and effects of ED	Interpersonal communication	Confidence to refer
Role of school personnel	With parents and students	
Referral sources available		
When to intercede		

These are the knowledge, skills, and attitudes regarding the
topic that the exemplary performer would possess following attendance at the seminar. We know the intended audience does not
have all of these characteristics based on earlier market research.
We cannot, however, assume that no one walking into the seminar
has any of these. So, the second step in the need assessment
process will be to determine which of these KSA characteristics
a typical audience member already possesses. The reason for
doing this, of course, is that no one wants to waste time on what
people already know.

Assessing which of these KSAs your intended audience already has can be done in the same ways you arrived at a picture
of your exemplar: your own experience, surveys of representa-

tives of your intended audience, other interested persons, job performance reviews, observation, and so forth. One cautionary note is necessary here. The value of self-reports is limited if you ask representatives of your intended audience which of these knowledge, skills, and attitudes they currently possess. Many will report that they possess most or all of them, yet you know from your own experience as well as other reports that in fact this is not true. These representatives of your intended audience are not lying; they simply believe better of themselves than objective sources would report. Use tests, skills demonstration, or observation of their current knowledge, skills, and attitudes on your topic to obtain objective measures. Also, consider using statistics that are already available. For example, what do statistics now show as the percentage of school personnel that refer students with eating disorders for outside help? If this figure is low, you will want to train participants on this topic during your workshop. Don't rule any of these out. Your choices should depend on time, resources, and subjects available. The results will be much more accurate.

Rarely, if ever, will you have a seminar audience which is completely homogeneous in terms of what they know about your topic. Our experience is that even when providing in-depth descriptions of who would benefit most from a seminar and setting explicit entrance requirements, audiences still end up dissimilar in many respects. This is not, of course, a bad thing except that it necessitates including a broader range of materials than you normally would so that no one is "left out" of the program. This means that some audience members will hear information they already know and others will hear less on a given subject than they truly need to hear. Our approach to a heterogeneous audience is usually to cover everything we have on our KSA list of the exemplar but to cover the areas most already know only at the most superficial levels.

By now you have determined a picture of the KSAs for your exemplar, and you have also created a picture of the KSAs of your intended audience members. The third step in this process is to contrast the two pictures. The difference between the two is the gap, and this gap will be the content of your workshop. This is what your audience will need to receive from you by the end of the seminar so they, too, will fit the picture of the exemplar. This gap should be fairly large or there is no need for your workshop. The gap reveals what you must include in your workshop and the degree of emphasis each area should receive.

Let's go back to our eating disorders example. Our assessment of the current status of our intended audience members revealed they

- already see eating disorders as a prevalent problem,
- don't believe they (school personnel) have the responsibility or right to get involved,
- have very little knowledge of symptoms or how to recognize them,
- believe they can't legally refer students,
- are unaware of most referral sources available,
- know some of the causes of eating disorders, and
- have had no communication with parents/physicians on this topic and said they would be uncomfortable talking about it.

This current picture differs greatly from the picture we created earlier of the exemplary educator who refers eating-disordered students. The difference between these two pictures tells us we must cover the following in our seminar:

- Review forms of eating disorders, causes, and effects
- Describe the symptoms and how to recognize them
- Emphasize the importance of school personnel's role in helping these students
- Clarify educators' legal rights to intervene
- Teach when and how to intercede
- Build skills in interpersonal communication with parents and physicians
- Familiarize participants with referral resources available and use of referral materials

From this list we arrive at an understanding of what we must cover in the workshop and in what detail. We have also learned the best way to approach these topics because of the audience's fears, beliefs, and/or biases.

WRITING EDUCATIONAL OBJECTIVES

The next step in the design process is to take what we have learned through need assessment and turn this information into learning objectives for the seminar. Learning objectives serve several purposes. For you, the seminar designer, these learning objectives tell you what you must accomplish with your audience during your seminar and what you must design into your seminar. They highlight the focal points of your program, and because learning objectives are written behaviorally, they provide the basis for your later evaluation of seminar effectiveness.

Behavioral learning objectives are not just for your benefit in designing the program, but they are also useful in marketing because they tell prospective audience members what they will learn during your seminar. They are a sales tool to use in promotional materials. When it comes to writing learning objectives, the mistake novices make most often is to not write them. Would-be seminar designers assume that statements from the need assessment will serve equally well, or they are satisfied with brief descriptions of content areas or subjects. Unfortunately, these statements are not focused enough. Consider the difference between the following: (a) Participants need to know more about the symptoms of eating disorders, versus (b) participants will be able to describe all the symptoms of three different eating disorders.

The second statement tells us our seminar must cover symptoms of all three eating disorders and, just as important, what behaviors we will expect on the part of participants to verify that this learning has occurred. For evaluation purposes, we will require participants at the conclusion of the program to *describe* symptoms of three eating disorders.

Learning objectives must be written behaviorally. By using behavioral language, we will be able to verify that the desired learning has occurred because behaviors are actions we can see, hear, or observe. Behaviors require no subjective judgments on our part; we either observe or do not observe the desired behavior.

There are a multitude of action verbs that are helpful in writing behavioral objectives. These include

describe	state	identify	list
explain	use	demonstrate	tell
show	model	administer	choose

Get in the habit (at least in your mind) of beginning each learning objective with the phrase "At the conclusion of this program participants will be able to . . ." (followed by your action verb). This will ensure that you are writing behavioral outcomes. Remember, behavior can be seen or heard. If you cannot see or hear something, you are probably not writing behaviorally. Steer clear of objectives which include phrases such as "understand" or "positive attitude." These cannot be seen or heard. They are not behaviors. They cannot be measured. Ask yourself what behavior you will see or hear if participants in your seminar understand or have positive attitudes. But if you ask them to "describe the value of . . ." or "list the four components of . . .," you will identify behavior that can be measured by anyone. The stunning advantage of these behavioral objectives is that they can be highlighted in your marketing efforts to demonstrate the benefits your program will offer.

Examples of poor learning objectives include

1. Participants will feel that CPR is a valuable life-saving skill.
2. A thorough understanding of fetal alcohol syndrome will be gained.
3. Learners can expect new relationships to open up for them.

These can better be written as behavioral learning objectives, such as

1. Participants will be able to state the reasons CPR is a valuable life-saving skill.

2. Participants will be able to explain causes and effects of fetal alcohol syndrome.
3. Participants will be able to initiate new social relationships.

It is also a characteristic of good behavioral learning objectives to be quantified when possible. Consider our previous three examples quantified:

1. Participants will be able to state three reasons CPR is a valuable life-saving skill.
2. Participants will be able to explain four causes and eight effects of fetal alcohol syndrome.
3. Participants will be able to initiate at least three new social relationships within 30 days.

Preparation of clear objectives or goals for your seminar serves several important purposes. The objectives serve as an outline of what you will try to accomplish and guide the preparation of the material in the modules that will form the substance of the seminar. Well-written objectives also serve an important role in marketing, specifically advertising. Here is where you will illustrate in a concrete way the benefits to be gained by attending your seminar. The people who read your brochure or flyer will sell themselves if you have clearly set out the benefits to be gained from attendance.

In this case, we will use the objectives we prepared for two different audiences on the topic of AD/HD to illustrate how the need assessment leads to the consideration of what benefits you want to tell your audience you will provide and how this in turn leads to the written objectives. Listed below are the objectives for psychologists and social workers who attend our seminar on children with Attention-Deficit/Hyperactivity Disorder. Participants in these seminars come in roughly equal numbers from schools and clinical settings.

At the completion of this conference participants will

1. identify the defining characteristics of Attention-Deficit/ Hyperactivity Disorder.

2. discuss the history and background information from home and the classroom relevant to a diagnosis of Attention-Deficit/Hyperactivity Disorder.
3. differentiate learned patterns of behavior, conduct disorder, and learning disability from those behavioral and learning problems that reflect symptoms of AD/HD.
4. list and describe the nature and action of psychostimulants, tranquilizers, and antidepressant drugs and their role in the management of children with Attention-Deficit/Hyperactivity Disorder.
5. state the pivotal role educators can often play in the co-ordination of medical treatment and school management.
6. relate the learning characteristics of children with AD/HD to practical issues of minuting discipline and development of curriculum in the classroom.
7. describe the natural course of development of AD/HD from preschool years through young adulthood along with practical implications this has for education planning.
8. tell about the impact of a child with AD/HD on classroom dynamics as well as on the function of the family.
9. list and describe a series of specific strategies and intervention techniques to improve behavior and enhance learning of children with AD/HD.
10. develop a comprehensive treatment plan that will address symptoms of AD/HD, including secondary psychological symptoms and family relationships.

Note that the objectives include several dealing with strategies to teach children and manage their behavior in the classroom. Why are these objectives included in a program for social workers and psychologists? Don't they belong in a seminar for teachers?

These objectives are included here because social workers and psychologists told us they needed this information. A substantial amount of their work involved consulting with parents and teachers who expected them to be knowledgeable about setting up behavior management programs in the classroom, knowledgeable about group dynamics in the classroom, able to give advice to keep conflict to a minimum, and knowledgeable about behavior intervention strategies appropriate for a classroom with many other students present.

As you would expect, the objectives for our AD/HD program for teachers include many objectives related to using an understanding of AD/HD to prepare curriculum materials and maintain behavior control within the classroom. There are also objectives dealing with group dynamics to help teachers deal with the complex relationships within the classroom and on the playground. But also included are the following:

1. Discuss the history and background information from home and the classroom relevant to a diagnosis of AD/HD.
2. Explain the use of educational, psychological, and medical tests in the diagnosis of AD/HD.
3. State the process of differential diagnoses especially as applied to the differentiation of AD/HD, Conduct Disorder, Oppositional Defiant Disorder, anxiety, depression, and learning disabilities.

Some of these objectives might surprise you, too. Many are the same as objectives for psychologists and social workers. To some extent that should not be surprising because any discussion of AD/HD has to cover most of the same material. But why does the workshop for teachers contain a section on diagnosis? Teachers do not diagnose medical or psychological disorders.

The section on diagnosis appears because in our surveys teachers told us they needed it, although not to make a diagnosis. Teachers are as aware as any professional about the boundaries of their expertise. They said they needed to know more about diagnosis because they are often asked for information by psychologists, family doctors, pediatricians, psychiatrists, and neurologists. They wanted to understand better the process of diagnosis so they could pass along what they knew in a way that would be most helpful. Teachers say they get a lot of inconsistent and contradictory requests from professionals examining their students. Some pediatricians ask for one thing, some for another. At times it seems to teachers that psychologists do not ask for what teachers think psychologists need and at other times teachers do understand why they are asked for something else. "Tell us what is going on," the teachers said. "Tell us about the process, who does what and why, and we will be in a better position to use our knowledge of children and what goes on in the classroom to give other professionals information that will be useful."

We often hear audience comments, such as, "It was seeing that you were going to talk about strategies for the classroom that convinced me to come," or "I decided to register because of the section on peer relationships of children with AD/HD." These people focused on only one or two of the objectives, but that was what made it worthwhile for them.

Understanding needs, *as perceived by the participants*, also helps you market more effectively. Let's take another look at one of our seminar titles: "Practical Strategies of Discipline for the Classroom." We chose the word "strategy" because it came up in every discussion with teachers. Strategy is the word teachers use to refer to techniques, methods, or procedures. We could have titled our program "Practical Techniques of Discipline for the Classroom," and it would have been a pretty good title, but it would have lost the edge that strikes a responsive chord in teachers.

Common sense might have led us to the word "practical" in our title, but, as valuable as common sense may be, it is not a substitute for research. We found that teachers complained a great deal about how the advice they received from outsiders was often too "theoretical" or did not take into consideration the day-to-day practical demands of the classroom. That's also why we used the word "classroom" in the title. We heard teachers express their concern that techniques (or even strategies) of discipline that they read about in books on behavior management often did not take into consideration the unique features of the classroom. We wanted them to know we understood.

It has been our experience that there is a need to understand the classroom and the practical restraints on teachers, such as large numbers of students and limited time to devote to any one child, but beyond that, the principles of behavior management are the same in the classroom, living room, or playground. We tried to make that clear to participants in our workshops in an effort to ensure that what they learned would have the broadest possible application. But, of course, you have to get them to attend the program in the first place, and you will get them to attend if you talk to them in their own language. Make it clear you will meet their needs as they perceive those needs, not as we define them.

Here is another example of responding to the needs of an audience. A plastic surgery group offered occasional public lectures to inform people about its practice. They hoped the lectures would yield larger patient volume for the group. Their initial efforts were successful in drawing an audience but not to the extent they had hoped. Trying to assess the reason for their limited success, they focused on how they presented the lecture topics to the public and realized they were depending on their own ideas of what the potential audiences (and potential patients) needed. They were close but not entirely on the mark. For example, one program was titled "Latest Developments in Laser Surgery That Allow Plastic Surgeons to Do Painless Scarless Surgery." Can you define the audience for this program? Is it people who want to know about laser surgery? Unlikely. How many people can there be in the lay public who would find a lecture on laser surgery of more than passing interest. Besides, they are not the audience the surgeons are seeking. More likely, this topic will appeal to people who already are considering surgery but are fearful of pain or scars. That makes more sense, but that is a limited audience that excludes many who have not yet come to the serious question, let alone a decision, about whether plastic surgery is for them.

The surgeons knew that plastic surgery was an optional procedure for most people and that they experienced a great deal of ambivalence. Ambivalence extended to the earliest stages of making an appointment and approaching the surgeon's office for an initial consultation. Recognizing the importance of decision making as a primary need in their potential audience, the lecture topics remained essentially the same, but the titles were modified to emphasize the assistance that would be offered (the benefit) in making all types of decisions regarding plastic surgery.

In this case, the surgeons kept their original title but added several subtitles in bold print to enhance their emphasis. "This program will answer questions such as, 'How do I decide whether I ought to consult a doctor in the first place?' 'How do I decide if plastic surgery might be right for me?' " The focus was placed on decision making with no sacrifice of the scientific content that the doctors also believed was important. But the patient's chief need was help in decision making and that benefit sold the program.

Finally, asking early audiences, "What questions or concerns did you hope to have answered by today's program?" revealed that a substantial number of people knew that most plastic surgery was a matter of personal choice and that, therefore, many insurance companies would not pay for the operation. It was a simple matter to add this topic to the advertising for the lecture. A brief sentence was added that stated that many plastic surgery operations were paid for by insurance and that the lecturer would be able to answer questions about insurance coverage.

DESIGNING THE MODULES

Once learning objectives have been written, the next step is to identify the content areas or modules for your seminar. Your seminar may have one or two content areas or a dozen or more. The number will reflect how many discrete subject areas are contained in your objectives. The content areas should be clear from reading your objectives.

There are many ways to accomplish each of your learning objectives and to design each of your modules. First, you will want to decide in what order you will present each of the modules you identified. Some elements of your program will have to follow a certain sequence. For example, background information, history, or definition of technical terms logically precede a summary of current information. But the organization and sequence of many of the elements of the seminar are a matter of your discretion. You will want to organize them in a way that is most likely to hold your audience's attention and is the most enjoyable for you. If you are presenting a half- or full-day program, it is important that you have chosen a design with the proper pace and variety to keep yourself interested and enthusiastic.

Once you have the outline for the full program, you will have to develop each module. Although the entire program must fit together, the actual writing and other preparation is accomplished in these modules. We recommend this "modular" design because modules designed for one seminar may be later used for other seminars, workshops, or classes. So, in essence, you will be designing "stand alone" pieces. Modules also can be moved around in the delivery of your workshop as needs and requirements change.

Adult Learning

Adults learn differently than children. Workshop design has to take this into consideration. Adults have a lifetime of experience to draw upon, so they learn best when their experience is used during the seminar. Adults demand respect. Disdain or condescension for the learner will interfere with learning. Adults learn best when they are involved in their own learning and have the opportunity to "do something" which helps integrate the learning. Using a variety of teaching and learning techniques will also facilitate adult learning. These elements stand in contrast with the traditional learning environment for children - which some would argue doesn't work very well for children, either. Yet, because many new seminar presenters are unfamiliar with adult learning theory, they make the mistake of trying to design a good workshop based on the only learning model they know - that which they, themselves, were exposed to as students. Usually that means the teacher talks and the students listen or answer questions.

The practical implications of all this for the development of your seminar are

- Ask participants about their expectations and try to meet as many expectations as possible.

- When you can't meet an expectation, explain why.
- Use a variety of training methods.
- Involve members of the audience in the teaching/learning process whenever possible.
- Require participants to act as partners in their own learning.
- State what participants can expect to get out of the workshop.
- Integrate participants' life experiences into the workshop design.

The design of workshop modules is a creative process. There is no one right way to design a module. There are many pathways to the learning goal(s) of each module. Your choice of format for each module will depend on many factors, such as the time available, location of the training, the type of audience, how well the audience knows each other, the number of people in the audience, costs, and, of course, the nature of your topic and the learning objectives for the topic. Trying to teach a group of 15 physical therapists a new technique for ambulating wheelchair-bound patients requires very different learning strategies than does trying to teach 150 managers from area corporations about the stresses their employees are experiencing in the 1990s.

Participants need not feel the experience was fun or pleasurable for learning to occur. A good deal of learning involves some discomfort as learners move out of the comfort zone, consisting of what they already know, into an area of uncertainty and the realization that there are things they do not know. This creates motivation to learn. There may be further discomfort trying out what is being learned. Until the new skill or idea is mastered, most learners experience a degree of discomfort. Don't design with entertainment in mind, although it need not be exclusive to effective learning. A creative teacher can make even the most tedious or difficult material interesting.

There are many teaching and learning techniques to consider. These include

discussion	drama
self-assessment	fill-in-the-blank
case studies	lectures/lecturettes
simulations	computer-based training
quizzes/tests	role play
games	outdoor/physical activities
music	small group tasks
audiotapes/videotapes	

Choose the format for each module that best fits your objectives. Use a variety of formats when possible. Look for opportunities to involve learners and to give them "hands-on" experience. Don't discard an idea you have because your first reaction is "It's too crazy" or "They'd never go for this." Remember that helping people learn often involves getting them out of familiar boxes. Imagine you are conducting a seminar for physicians, and your first idea involves the use of role play. You immediately tell yourself that a group of physicians wouldn't go for the idea of being involved in a drama, and you are ready to discard your idea. Stop! Before you discard the idea, consider whether the benefits of using this training format outweigh the costs. How does role play fit with the rest of your seminar modules? Is it the best way for participants to learn the substance of this particular module? Do you have the time, room, and necessary materials to do it? Be creative and stretch as you design your workshop. Think back to the courses, workshops, and classes you have attended and what learning strategies enhanced your own learning. Remember the features you were skeptical about but found effective.

You should consider the time of day you have planned for each module as well as where it fits in the total scheme. As in any presentation, the introductory period is crucial. This is the point where many participants will decide they love or hate this seminar, and it will be difficult to dislodge this impression later. Therefore, you should attempt to do something interesting or exciting that will positively color their perception of the remainder of the day. It is often a good idea to do something early in the seminar day that gets people involved. This makes clear that you expect them to be active and involved and are not doing this program alone. Furthermore, involving participants early on will give you an opportunity to set a supportive, positive tone by affirming the contributions members of the audience make.

Be careful of the time after lunch. This is not the time to darken the room and show a videotape. The time immediately before the day's end is also risky. People are tired. Some are thinking about slipping out a bit early. You must design something here that is certain to hold the audience's interest, preferably something that actively involves them. Plan question/answer periods at specific points in the seminar. Questions taken throughout the program tend to be disruptive. Plan breaks in the program. People need an opportunity to get up and move around. They also need to be able to use the restrooms.

As you design each module, create a *Facilitator's Guide* for your own use. This is a step-by-step guide for you or another presenter to follow when delivering each module. Creating this guide is part of your design process. The guide should describe the following for each module:

- Name of module
- Learning objectives for that module
- Chronological outline of module
- Lecture notes
- Statement of the purpose for each activity
- Step-by-step directions for each activity
- Materials needed for activity
- Time estimates
- Alternatives/Options available
- Suggestions to encourage discussion if desired

While everything here is necessary for the presenter, we cannot stress enough the need to give your audience clear directions for any activities you plan. Directions that are confusing will negate any possible learning you intended from the module, and unclear directions will seriously undermine your credibility. These potential trouble areas as well as the effort involved are what encourages some seminar leaders to fall back on lectures as the sole format used for their seminar. But it's tough to listen to someone give a 6-hour speech (or even one that lasts 2 hours) so unless you are an extraordinary speaker, your seminar has to include a little variety.

As you design your workshop, don't forget handout materials. Whether for use during your program or for reference later, participants want and expect handout materials. The quantity and quality of this material is expected to go up as the price you charge goes up. Handouts can provide backup for what you offer in the seminar or supplement information recall after the program. References also make good handouts. Make your handouts appear as professional as possible. If you plan to include reproductions of articles in print, be certain to obtain written permission from the copyright holder - not the author - first.

EVALUATION

The final step in the design of your seminar is the creation of a means to evaluate your seminar. Evaluation is essential because the results provide you with feedback on its effectiveness. You can make a course correction if you are slightly off track. If you do any work presenting seminars for businesses or other large institutions, they will certainly expect an evaluation of the effectiveness of the program. More and more organizations are aware of the high cost of continuing education and training, so you will be held accountable to show the value received from your seminar or workshop. Finally, an evaluation gives your participants an opportunity to be heard. Most seminar participants expect this and would complain if no opportunity for evaluation were allowed.

There are four levels of seminar evaluation. There are reasons for each level and uses for the feedback from each. You must know your goals before you decide how to evaluate the effectiveness of your seminar. Many people collect information for which they have no use, so think about what you are going to do with the information you obtain. The first level of evaluation is the one we are all familiar with and the one that is easiest to accomplish. It also provides the most superficial information which is often of little use. Level one evaluation refers to assessment of participants' reactions. We ask people whether they liked the program or what they thought about different aspects of it. Was the content interesting? Did it meet their needs? How were the facilities? What did they think about the seminar leader? How helpful were the handouts? This is not entirely useless. You want to know what participants thought or felt about your program. Their reactions are important in terms of whether they would attend another of your programs or recommend your programs to a friend or colleague. These reactions do not, however, tell you whether anyone learned anything. Nonetheless, this type of evaluation would fit the bill just fine if your goal was to introduce yourself or your practice to the audience with an eye toward encouraging them to follow up with you in your office.

The second level of evaluation does assess what participants have learned. This involves the use of some form of testing. Testing can be in the form of a paper-and-pencil test, skill demonstrations, or oral questions and answers. These tests are normally conducted at the conclusion of the workshop.

Evaluations conducted at levels three and four are more difficult to accomplish and are often neglected. Level three and four evaluations, however, yield the most meaningful information. A level three evaluation assesses behavioral change. What behavior of participants changed as a result of the training or seminar? An evaluation of this sort can be conducted at the conclusion of the program and/or at a later time to assess long-term learning. Remember our insistence on writing learning objectives in behavioral terms? One significant reason is found here in the evaluation process. Those behavioral learning objectives tell us exactly what behavior to look for in order to evaluate course effectiveness.

Finally, an evaluation at level four determines the *results* obtained as a consequence of attending our seminar. What difference was achieved for children, patients, employees, the system, or the organization? This level of evaluation provides answers to the question "So what?" Did a savings in a certain number of employee work hours result from this training? How much money was saved? How many lives were saved? How many more customers were satisfied? How many fewer instances of spouse abuse occurred? What was the improvement in student achievement?

This is the most significant form of evaluation and the most difficult to obtain. Unless you are working with an entire system, whether it be a family system or a large organization, you will not be able to conduct this level of evaluation.

Your choice of which level(s) of evaluation to obtain depends entirely on what information you have use for. With a new seminar, you may be very concerned with how participants felt about the day. You want their immediate reactions because you will use this information in considering where to modify your program. But you may also want quantifiable data on what learning took place or what behavior change occurred so you can use the information to sell your program to others.

Chapter 4
Marketing Your Seminar I

"Marketing has far more to do with business success than quality or any other factor," says Herman Holtz, author of *Expanding Your Consulting Practice With Seminars* (1987, p. 7). We agree. Of course, the quality of your program is important, but, no matter how good you are, people will not know it until they hear you, and people will not see and hear you until you persuade them to attend your seminar. Many good ideas and well-developed programs fail because of inadequate or misdirected marketing efforts.

Marketing is more than just selling or advertising. Marketing encompasses everything you do to bring your product or service to your patients, clients, or customers. From the name you choose for your practice group or agency to the design of your letterhead and the words your receptionist uses to answer the phone, all are part of marketing. It includes the concepts you develop, the name you give your seminar, the way you present it to your potential audience, and how you provide sales and advertising information to that audience. The earlier you incorporate notions of marketing into your seminar planning the more effective and productive you will be.

Over the years a reputation for excellence will help sell seminars, but a good reputation will never be enough, especially if you develop a national schedule of seminars. Reputations are usually local and fleeting. Moreover, no matter how good a service or product may be, how will anyone find out about it? How do you know about the quality of a book, seminar, movie, automobile, university program, singer, orchestra, or art museum? Usually it is because of marketing efforts that have stressed the high level of quality as a main feature of the program or article being sold to you.

But Holtz also points out that allegations of quality have little effect on actual sales or, in our case, attendance at our seminars. This shouldn't surprise you. After all, people expect advertising to stress the quality of a product, and when we read glowing testimonials we generally take such information with a large grain of salt. Indeed, we would be surprised at an advertisement that did not tell us how wonderful something was. In a sense, statements about high quality actually homogenize advertising so no single item stands out. There are exceptions, and arguments about quality are not without some merit, but very few people will find your promise of high quality a compelling reason to attend your seminar.

So why does anyone decide to attend a seminar, and what can you do to make sure it will be your seminar they attend? Now, discussing marketing, we return to a subject raised earlier; the people who are potential registrants at your seminar must believe your product will meet a need they recognize they have. Your advertising and other promotional material have to highlight that need and show that you have a product that will provide a benefit.

Typically, people buy a benefit, not a service or a thing or even technology. Always stress the benefit to be gained. Few people will attend a seminar on new developments in the treatment of anxiety disorders just because they are curious about the topic. They will attend because they expect a benefit, and it is your job to understand what benefits they are looking for and then design your promotional materials in a way that convinces them you can deliver. For example, the benefit for someone suffering from an intractable anxiety disorder is the possibility of relief from symptoms, and that is why that individual will attend the seminar. A professional, on the other hand, may perceive the benefit to be learning new techniques that he or she will be able to apply in his or her professional practice. Similarly, "How to Tell Whether Your Child's Behavior Problem Requires Professional Attention" makes clear the benefit in a way that the title "Childhood Behavior Disorders" does not.

DEVELOPING PROMOTIONAL MATERIALS

Since market research and need assessment was part of the process used to select and develop a seminar topic, you have already done the preliminary marketing that will lead now to developing promotional material. The seminar title and the text of brochures, flyers, and other advertising will follow directly from what you have learned as you assessed your market earlier.

The purpose of promotional material is two-fold. First, it has to capture the reader's attention. If there is not enough in the first line or first glance to make the reader want to move to the second line, you will not be able to sell your seminar. And you have to keep readers' attention so they read all, or at least enough, of the brochure to arrive at what is your second purpose: a clear explanation of what benefits will be gained from attending your seminar.

We learned a sobering lesson when we started offering seminars. Many people who attended our seminars had not read the entire brochure or flyer - after all the work we put into it! They may have read nothing more than the title and subtitle and the registration form. In every case we had provided a course outline, objectives, and a narrative description of the program that set out in detail what would be covered. We remain convinced that we did a good job, but some people never read the text or examined the outline.

We can only speculate about why people read selectively, but the lesson to learn is that you cannot be sure what thoughts, knowledge, and experience people will bring with them when they attend your seminar. Similarly, we must assume that there are plenty of people who see a brochure and decide to not attend a seminar but who are as mistaken in that notion as are the people who wind up attending and find they are out of their element. They most likely registered because the title or subtitle or first sentence, or whatever it was that they did read, convinced them the program would meet their needs. Unfortunately for some people, we were not going to meet their needs because we did not know what these needs were and they had not read what we were going to do.

But we gained useful information from the experience. It emphasized the vital importance of being absolutely certain that whatever message we wanted to get across to attract our audience had to be available in a very brief statement and easily accessible on the first page of our brochure. By all means, write your advertising material as if potential registrants will devour every word, but you will more likely persuade readers that you have something especially good to offer if your points are brief and clear. We have to write to keep the reader interested enough to want to find out what comes next. And many who encounter your promotional material will read all or most of it if you initially capture their attention. But you cannot count on your reader sticking it out to the very end.

For this reason we use the inverted-pyramid style of writing for all our advertising copy. This is the style usually used by newspaper reporters. A reporter may get an assignment to write a 500-word article. However, by the time all the articles are written and the page is set out, the editor usually finds that some articles need more space and others may have to be added at the last minute, so some stories have to be shortened. Editors rarely have time to rewrite anything, and there is usually no time to ask the reporter to write a shorter article. The solution to this problem is the inverted pyramid. Critical information goes in the first sentence or two. Other facts and descriptions essential to understanding the main point of the article go into the next few sentences. Less vital information goes next, along with details and quotes and examples that may be interesting but could be sacrificed if the article is too long. An editor can begin cutting the article just by snipping off sentences, or even whole paragraphs, from the end without destroying the essential information of the article. In fact, in an ideal article a reader could get enough information from only the first sentence to at least get the general idea of the story.

So it should be with what you write. Assume everyone will read the first sentence. That is usually your title. After that you can't be sure.

There is a common adage in direct mail marketing: "The more you tell, the more you sell," suggesting the more you can cram into an envelope the greater your prospects of interesting someone in what you are selling. To us that seems like emphasizing quantity over quality. We've heard and read a lot of opinions about how to attract readers to one sheet of paper after another and keep their attention so they will devour your sales literature. It's a great idea, so if we knew a way to write our own sales literature so anyone who opens the mail will read three or four densly typewritten pages, we would certainly do it. We just don't know how, and we think it is a mistaken idea. Besides, you don't need research here because you have your own experience and common sense to guide you. How many hundreds of envelopes filled with advertising have you opened and how often have you read all the material they contained? Our experience has taught us that most people will spend very little time to examine your material. You had better explain quickly and succinctly what you are offering and why your reader needs you.

There are two essential elements to your sales literature, the elements you count on to make the sale. Other features may be important, but markedly less so. The first key element is the title. The title is the first thing most people see. If your title does not capture readers' interest, it is unlikely they will read further. The second element is a list of objectives for the course which will tell the reader what needs of theirs you will meet, what benefits you will provide. "What's in it for me?" they will ask. "Why should I invest my time and money?"

All the rest is window dressing and administrative detail. Make it nice and pretty if you can, but if you have failed to capture the readers' attention with your title or failed to answer the basic question of benefits, you will not make the sale with window dressing.

Brochures and Flyers

You will probably use different types of promotional materials for your seminar, but the one you will use most is a brochure or flyer. The precise form of the brochure will differ from program to program and from market to market though we usually use a small brochure that unfolded is 8½ by 11 inches, the standard size for letterhead and typewriter paper. We vary the color, quality of paper, design of the text, and sometimes color of ink, depending on the nature of the particular seminar we are offering, but only in exceptional circumstances do we make other major changes.

There isn't just one right way to design promotional material. Use any design that is effective, but usually you find what works only through trial and error. Still, there are some common sense guidelines that can save you a lot of trouble. You must expose your ideas to the critical eyes of others. Many of us are cautious when we start any new project, leery of telling others about our ideas lest they criticize and discourage us. You have to solicit others' opinions, especially when you design promotional materials. There is a need for balance. Too little advice denies you the benefit of the thoughts of others. Too much advice may get you bogged down in self-doubt and second guessing so you stall before you build up enough momentum to carry yourself along. You know yourself best. You know which of these mistakes you are more likely to make. If a critical decision has to be made and you have conflicting advice, remember you are the expert. Your judgment should prevail.

For example, several design consultants told us that the three-fold brochure we use most often is the worst form of brochure they could imagine. They said it lacked professional quality. Even when we insisted we wanted to use it they wanted us to change it. We thought the changes they suggested had little merit. Admittedly, we were anxious about rejecting advice from experts who not only should know what they are talking about but who were giving us the advice we had paid for. In the final analysis no one was ever able to give us any rationale or data in their argument against the three-fold brochure we liked. The design experts could only offer their opinion that "So many seminars were advertised using similar brochures that ours lacked an element of professionalism and a distinguishing punch." That was almost a persuasive argument because we offered good programs and we wanted to make sure no one got the wrong idea because the brochure we used was second rate. But our experience told us it worked.

For example, the brochure we use for our programs on Attention-Deficit/Hyperactivity Disorder appears on pages 84-85. Most of the brochures for our other programs follow a similar design. We prefer this format and design for three reasons. First, it is inexpensive. Our chief market for this program is educators, and there are nearly 12 million of them in the United States. So we have to send out large volumes of advertising. Even though we usually target only a portion of one state for each program, we are still talking about tens of thousands of teachers. So getting a lot of flyers for our printing dollar stood high on our list of priorities. For the same reason, we wound up using a moderate grade of paper.

Second, this simple, single-page flyer weighs very little. We can put a lot of them into an envelope and still keep our postage costs down. We are guided by the consideration of what the total cost is to put one of our brochures into the hands of a potential registrant. The delivery mechanism is often more expensive than the brochure itself, so think ahead when you design promotional material.

The third reason we use this design is that we believe it is our best chance to get a large place on bulletin boards in offices, clinics, and schools. Most three-fold flyers have the pages oriented along the short axis of the paper. When it is folded the print runs down the short side of the paper. The title and other important information in such a flyer can be seen only if the fully folded flyer is placed on the bulletin board. We counted on getting three times as much "shelf space" with our design. A four-

ATTENTION-DEFICIT/HYPERACTIVITY DISORDER
A WORKSHOP FOR PSYCHOLOGISTS, SOCIAL WORKERS, NURSES, COUNSELORS, AND TEACHERS
EMPHASIS OF <u>PRACTICAL</u> AND <u>REALISTIC</u> MANAGEMENT
STRATEGIES FOR SCHOOL AND HOME

THIS IS FOR PARENTS, TOO

PRESENTED BY EDUCATIONAL DEVELOPMENT CENTER
&
RONALD J. FRIEDMAN, PhD and PENNY ALTMAN, MA

WEDNESDAY, APRIL 5, 1997	THURSDAY, APRIL 6, 1997	FRIDAY, APRIL 7, 1997
8:30 a.m. - 3:15 p.m.	8:30 a.m. - 3:15 p.m.	8:30 a.m. - 3:15 p.m.
(Registration 8:00 - 8:30 a.m.)	(Registration 8:00 - 8:30 a.m.)	(Registration 8:00 - 8:30 a.m.)
Lunch Noon - 1:00 p.m.	Lunch Noon - 1:00 p.m.	Lunch Noon - 1:00 p.m.
SHERATON INN	THE LANDMARK INN	HOLIDAY INN - TOTOWA
195 Highway 18	Routes 73 & 38	One Route 46 West
EAST BRUNSWICK, NEW JERSEY	MAPLE SHADE, NEW JERSEY	TOTOWA, NEW JERSEY

Attention-Deficit/Hyperactivity Disorder (AD/HD) causes a substantial number of behavior and learning problems. Unfortunately, AD/HD often goes unrecognized.

Attention-Deficit/Hyperactivity Disorder is probably the most frequently misunderstood and improperly diagnosed condition encountered by those working in the schools. Failure to complete homework, underachievement, immaturity, learning disabilities, and a variety of other behavioral and emotional problems often are symptoms of an underlying AD/HD. Proper understanding and diagnosis leading to appropriate programming and management are of utmost importance.

This workshop is based on our experience with over 1,000 children with Attention-Deficit/Hyperactivity Disorder. Following participation in this workshop you will be better able to identify children with Attention-Deficit/Hyperactivity Disorders and work with them more effectively. Information about the learning characteristics of AD/HD children will be reviewed and specific practical applications of these findings for child management and development of educational strategies in regular and special education classrooms will be presented.

The workshop also includes discussion of medication and a review of medical management of AD/HD with an emphasis on the coordination of school and medical treatment.

Certificates for Teacher Education Credit and Nursing CEU provided. Call for an update on other CEU credit.

REGISTRATION & FEE: $55.00 (Lunch is on your own). School or Agency purchase orders can be accepted for 5 or more registrants. If registration form below has already been used, mail your name and address with a check for the registration fee to

Educational Development Center, ATTN: Maureen Dermer
904 E. Old Willow Road, #102 ● Prospect Heights, IL 60070 ● (501) 671-6611

Please Make Check Payable to RONALD J. FRIEDMAN, PhD

....

I WILL ATTEND (CIRCLE ONE)　　EAST BRUNSWICK　　MAPLE SHADE　　TOTOWA

NAME _____ PHONE _____

ADDRESS _____

CITY _____ STATE _____ ZIP _____

Psychologist ___　Social Worker ___　Teacher ___　Physician ___　Nurse ___　Other _____

Educational Development Center
904 E. Old Willow Road, #102
Prospect Heights, IL 60070

ATTENTION-DEFICIT/HYPERACTIVITY DISORDER COURSE OBJECTIVES:

At the completion of this conference, participants will

- Be familiar with a series of specific strategies and intervention techniques to improve behavior and enhance learning of child with AD/HD

- Be able to identify the defining characteristics of Attention-Deficit/Hyperactivity Disorder

- Be familiar with history and background information from home and the classroom relevant to a diagnosis of Attention-Deficit/Hyperactivity Disorder

- Be able to differentiate learned patterns of behavior, conduct disorder, and learning disability from those behavioral and learning problems that reflect symptoms of AD/HD

- Be familiar with the nature and action of psychostimulants, tranquilizers, and antidepressant drugs and their role in the management of children with Attention-Deficit/Hyperactivity Disorder

- Understand the pivotal role educators can often play in the coordination of medical treatment and school management

- Learn the salient features of learning characteristics of children with Attention-Deficit/Hyperactivity Disorder with respect to response to reinforcement schedules, contingency reinforcement, and other features of learning

- Be able to relate the learning characteristics of children with AD/HD to practical issues of maintaining discipline and development of curriculum in the classroom

- Understand the natural course of the development of AD/HD from the preschool years through young adulthood along with the practical implication this has for educational planning

- Gain further understanding of the impact of a child with Attention-Deficit/Hyperactivity Disorder on classroom dynamics as well as on the functioning of the family

- Be able to develop a comprehensive treatment plan that will address symptoms of AD/HD including secondary psychological symptoms and family relationship problems

Dr. Ronald Friedman is a child psychologist. He has been Assistant Professor of Pediatrics at the University of Iowa College of Medicine and Associate Professor in the Department of Applied Psychology at the University of Toronto and the Ontario Institute for Studies in Education. He is on the consulting staff of the Department of Pediatrics at St. John Hospital in Detroit and a consultant to special education departments in numerous school districts. He is the author of over 40 articles published in medical, psychology, and educational journals. He is also co-author of the books *Attention Deficit Disorder and Hyperactivity* and *Management of Children and Adolescents With Attention Deficit Hyperactivity Disorder*. Copies of Dr. Friedman's books and tapes will be available for sale.

EAST BRUNSWICK

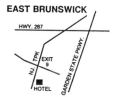

MAPLE SHADE

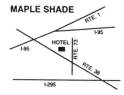

TOTOWA

Penny Altman, MA, has worked as a training and development professional for the past 15 years. Currently working as an independent consultant, she previously was employed by Allstate Insurance Company for 7 years, where she was responsible for major organizational change, team building, and management development. Her clients have included such diverse organizations as Intel, the American Bar Association, and local school districts. In addition, Ms. Altman has taught both graduate and undergraduate level classes in the areas of Communication, Management, Organization Development, and Training.

page brochure, slicker paper, different use of the paper, and different format all seemed to sacrifice something without providing a benefit.

We do use other formats, different designs, and different paper but only in selected instances. For instance, we use higher quality paper and extra color for brochures advertising the seminar based on this book. We usually target a smaller number of people, sometimes only a tenth as many as for one of our programs on discipline strategies, Attention-Deficit/Hyperactivity Disorder, or stress management. In addition, the people we want to reach are usually more sophisticated, at least in the sense that they have more experience with seminars and continuing education programs. Simply put, they have seen more flyers and sampled more merchandise. We want our offering to meet their expectations.

Writing Attention-Getting Copy

This will be your biggest challenge. Fortunately it is an area where friends, colleagues, and members of your prospective audience can be the most helpful. Make liberal use of them. When you ask people to comment on what you have written, do not tell them what you are trying to say or what you have in mind. Let your writing speak for itself. That is the way it will be when your prospect picks up the brochure and starts to read. You will not be there to explain "what you were trying to get at." After the draft of your brochure has been read, ask your readers to tell you what the copy said to them. Only then, ask pointed questions. Listen carefully to the answers. Then, finally, it is time to tell them what you were trying to say. If they did not "get it" before, see if they can recognize your message in the copy now. Ask why it was not clear the first time. Some of your readers will be able to give you insightful answers, and others will not. Try a few more people. It is inexpensive valuable research. Rewrite and try again. You will finally get copy that not only says what you mean but packs the punch you hope for.

Make sure several people who know nothing about your specialty read the copy to see if it makes sense. You are appealing to a knowledgeable audience, but your promotional material should be understandable by any educated layperson. Only they will be able to identify jargon that you and your colleagues have come to take for granted and may think is part of the language of the general public.

Be cautious using words or phrases that enjoy transient popularity, such as co-dependent, enabling, or adult children of alcoholics. These may be useful words or phrases, and you may want to include them, but do so judiciously. These expressions are examples of useful clinical concepts that have been adopted by lay readers and writers in popular magazines and extended to the point where little of the precision of their original meaning remains. If you use them, your brochure may say what you mean it to say but will also carry all the implications associated with "pop psych" words from recent articles in magazines and newspapers which may be more of a burden than you want to carry. Of course, your audience may be adult children of alcoholics or deal with the problems of enabling spouses of substance abusers, and the words may have a legitimate place in your promotional material. Just recognize the care you should take to ensure that your intended meaning matches with what readers will understand from what you have written.

Writing good copy is a skill, of course, and no one can teach a skill by offering advice on a printed page. As with any skill, writing develops as you write and get feedback from a supervisor or editor. Just as the best way to learn to interview, do psychotherapy, or sew up a wound is just to do it, so it is with writing. The way to learn to write is to write. Most people would probably write better if they could forget a lot of what was drummed into their heads in school about effective writing. Excessive attention to the classic elements of writing such as punctuation and carefully set out paragraphs gets in the way of many novice writers because they cannot concentrate on formal features of "good" writing and get their message across in a clear, succinct, and assertive manner. (Of course, following rules of grammar is important, but the primary objective in good writing is clarity of expression, not proper grammar, good penmanship, or a well-thought-out thesis sentence.)

Write as simply and as clearly as you can, avoiding jargon. Write quickly with whatever comes to mind. Get it down on paper. Don't worry about the quality of your sentences, the words you choose, the grammar, or the spelling. Don't even worry about whether it makes sense. Get it out of your head and onto paper. Few people write with ease; most find it difficult. Remember to "Banish the critic." Don't listen to the voice in your head that says what you just wrote does not make sense or what you just said contradicts what you said a few sentences back. Don't go back and correct your grammar or misspelling; that is just a delaying tactic. Translate your ideas into words on paper. Then edit what you wrote. Now you *do* have to pay attention to the sense of your effort, to grammar and spelling. In your first rewrite, try to clean up the clutter. Turn your clumsy or agrammatical prose into something sensible. Reorganize and write the transition sentences that help your copy hang together.

For your third draft you ought to be looking at the impact of what you have written. Writing clearly is primary, but you want to have a strong impact, too. "The train slowed down and stopped" tells what happened. "The train glided to a stop" says it better. Be alert for verbal clutter. Clutter dulls the impact of a sentence. We could have written, "It is very important to be alert for verbal clutter." Would that have had more impact? Of course not. The shorter sentence works best. But it is not just brevity that counts. Many of us have speech habits that include a large number of unimportant words. That matters less in speech because we can use volume, intensity, and diction to emphasize important points. You don't have that advantage with a printed page. Go through your copy and cut ruthlessly.

Show instead of tell. You are better off demonstrating your point than telling about it. "This program will be very helpful for the classroom teacher," is not going to convince anyone of the value of your seminar. Show how it will be helpful by using plain words to describe the knowledge and skills participants will take with them at the end of the day. Let the readers come to their own conclusions that this will be helpful because you have explained so well what benefits will accrue to them.

Choose strong nouns and verbs. Avoid adjectives and adverbs when possible. Cut out intensifiers. Intensifiers are usually adverbs but may also be adjectives. They are words you may think strengthen your argument, but they do not; they only dilute what you say. For example, "Our seminar will present very important new research findings." The word "very" in the preceding sentence is an intensifier. Does it add anything to the sentence? You have a limited amount of space in a brochure. Save it for something that matters.

The brochure that gets attention is one that has a title that captures readers' interest and stresses the benefit to be gained by attending the seminar. These are not separate elements. Both often occur together. For example, the words "How to" in the title "How to Develop, Design, and Market a Seminar for Health Care Professionals" incorporate both elements.

Using Testimonials

Testimonials can be an effective part of your marketing effort, but you have to be careful. They represent a double-edged sword. Used judiciously for specific reasons, they can be persuasive. But used in scatter-shotgun fashion, anonymously announcing how wonderful you are, they may cheapen your brochure and work against your best interests.

There are several types of testimonials. If you can obtain a brief statement from someone of great prominence praising your work, it does not matter much what they say as long as it is positive. You probably won't get many like that. Avoid using anonymous quotes if you can. Most people who give you a quote will give you permission to use their name. Use their credentials and their professional work affiliation if you can. Remember your reader is looking at all this with the question in his or her mind, "What's in this for me?" If your testimonial comes from a school teacher, but your reader is a clinical social worker in a psychiatric hospital, how much relevance will the quote have? "Dr. Jones was a witty and entertaining speaker" or "Dr. Winkowski was clearly well informed on the seminar topic" are okay, but they will not persuade anyone to attend your program.

The best testimonials stress the benefits attendance will confer. These are better: "Penny Altman helped me understand what has held me back from starting my own seminar. I know I will be able to get started now." "Dr. Friedman explained how Attention-Deficit/Hyperactivity Disorder causes problems in the classroom in a way that helped me plan more effective management strategies." "Ms. Mayer gave us a half-dozen tips that helped us save a lot of money advertising our programs."

Use the Marketing Brochure Checklist on pages 97-98 to review the design of your marketing brochure.

THE DIRECT MAIL CAMPAIGN

Most seminars are promoted by direct mail advertising because it is most effective and efficient. You can target your promotion campaign and keep costs under control with a better cost-effective rate of response than with any other strategy. And there are certain wrinkles you can take advantage of which allow even greater cost reductions in certain circumstances. We use other promotion strategies, too, but direct mail is the backbone of our efforts.

Mailing Lists

If you have not used mailing lists or direct mail campaigns before, they can seem intimidating. But there are many straightforward applications of the process, and there are many services available, such as mailing list brokers, who can direct you, at no charge, to the companies that sell exactly what you want. You can buy mailing lists or make your own. Surprisingly, homemade lists are often more expensive. Homemade lists are comprised of patients' or clients' names from your files and are probably cheapest, but names and addresses of individuals or institutions gathered from phone books or professional directories can be costly. While there is minimal expense obtaining these names, there is considerable cost involved in addressing envelopes or typing the names into a computer mailing list. Whether you choose to do this depends on how often you will use the list you generate and how much time and other resources you have at your disposal. Many beginners waste a lot of time compiling lists this way under the mistaken assumption that it is less expensive than buying names. Commercial companies that specialize in mailing lists and/or professional associations or state licensing authorities that have lists of all licensed professionals in the state will sell you names usually at modest prices.

For example, in 1996 we purchased the names of psychiatrists, psychologists, social workers, and marriage and family counselors in a three-county area of a state in the Midwest. The area included a large city, so there were about 9,700 names and addresses on the list. We bought the list from the State Department of Licensing and Professional Regulation for $56.10. But we wanted the names printed on peel-and-stick labels that could be easily affixed to the brochure or an envelope. "No problem," they said. We bought 10,000 labels at an office supply store for $125 and sent them to the licensing department; for no additional charge, they printed the list right on the labels.

Several years ago we wasted a lot of time and money although, at the time, we thought we were efficient. We intended to do a series of programs in several large- and medium-sized cities and wanted to reach as many social service agencies, government affiliated social service and mental health agencies, and privately practicing mental health workers as possible. We also wanted to mail to a number of other groups, including some that were not clearly defined or did not exist in numbers large enough so we could secure their names from our usual mailing list brokers. So we called the phone company and asked for yellow and white pages for each of these cities and surrounding areas. The phone company charges for the books, but you can get anything you want. Directories for larger cities are available at most public libraries for less than $200. You can buy computer tapes or discs that supply phone numbers for the entire country. These lists are cumbersome, however, and often out of date by the time you buy them.

We hired temporary staff to search the phone books and collate names, addresses, and phone numbers. By the time we were finished, we had a terrific mailing list. We were quite pleased with ourselves until, about 6 months later, we learned there are several mailing list brokers that specialize in gathering names from phone books. You provide them with the categories you want, and they will give you complete lists on paper, tape, discs, peel-off labels, whatever you want, within 3 to 5 days at a fraction of the cost of doing it yourself. Use a mailing list broker when you don't have a clear picture in your mind of what you are looking for. While many mailing list brokers sell lists themselves, their main service is to be familiar with many different list providers and serve as a consultant or intermediary to help you find the mailing list company that best meets your needs. The brokers earn their commission from the companies that sell lists, so they help you narrow down your choices; it will not cost you anything. They will help clarify your needs and then put you in touch with the list companies who can sell you the lists if the brokers them-selves cannot. Our lists usually cost about $50 per thousand names.

There are other ways to obtain mailing lists if you would rather put in the time yourself and save some money. For example, the least expensive way to obtain the names of school principals and addresses of schools is to buy a directory from Market Data Research (MDR), a subsidiary of Dun and Bradstreet. They sell a directory, updated every year, of each state's schools and school districts, including all private schools The cost is about $50 per state. They will also provide directories of preschools and col-leges and universities sorted by academic interest, department, and so on. Then you prepare your own labels although MDR also sells labels. If you anticipate using the same list over and over, you should buy the directory and pay to have a computerized list made that you can then print over and over again at minimal cost. If you anticipate only a single use, it is often less expensive just to buy the labels.

Similar resources exist for hospitals, mental health clinics, multispecialty medical clinics, physical therapists, nurses, audiolo-gists, speech therapists, social workers, or anyone else you might want to contact. Subscriber lists for professional journals, and membership lists for professional organizations, as well as state licensing authorities, are good sources. Keep in mind all the professions related to yours when you are attempting to make a list of resources. We have included a few mailing list houses, mailing list brokers, and other resources below.

**Marketing and
Continuing Education Resources**

Mailing Lists

American Business Lists
P.O. Box 27347
57075 S. 86th Circle
Omaha, NE 68127-4146
Telephone: 402-331-7169
Business lists from yellow pages

PPM Marketing
999 Eighteenth Street
Suite 2420
Denver, CO 80202-2424
Telephone: 800-221-0223
Seminar specialists

Market Data Retrieval
16 Progress Drive
Box 2117
Shelton, CT 06484-9990
Telephone: 800-243-5538
Schools and libraries

Mailing List Broker

Burnett Marketing, Inc.
800 Lee Street, Suite 6
Des Plaines, IL 60016-6446
Telephone: 708-803-2727
*Specializes in seminars and
  courses*

Direct Marketing

Direct Marketing Association
Bette Lawler
11 W. 42nd Street
New York, NY 10036-8096
Telephone: 212-768-7277
*Books and resources on
  marketing*

Resource for Offering Continuing Education Credit

International Association of
  Continuing Education and Training
1200 19th Street NW
Suite 300
Washington, DC 20036-2401
Telephone: 202-857-1122
*Approves seminar companies to
  offer CEUs*

Two additional references you will find useful are *The Complete Direct Marketing Source Book* by John Kremer (1992) and *Direct Mail List Rates and Data* (1992). The latter book may be in your local library; any local mailing list broker will surely have a copy. It is a list of lists, explaining where the lists are compiled from, how to order, costs, and other information needed to choose.

It is easier to reach people who are part of an institution, whether a business, hospital, clinic, or member of an association, because these people will have their names on mailing lists already. Or you can reach them through their association or employer. If your potential audience is made up of individuals from the general population, you may still find a mailing list broker helpful. They will be able to provide lists of names categorized by type of person you want to reach. For example, you should be able to get a list of people with a post-high school education, living within certain zip codes, who have taken a self-improvement course from a college, continuing education, or seminar provider in the past 2 years. The more esoteric your needs become, the less likely you will be able to find carefully targeted lists. In these circumstances consider other means of advertising such as newspaper ads, radio spot announcements, or notices in other local publications.

Use of the Mail

We usually use a combination of special 4th-class mail and first-class mail. First-class mail is expensive, but we are convinced that a business size envelope with a first-class stamp delivered into someone's hand is less likely to be consigned unread to the waste paper basket than an obvious piece of bulk mail that literally screams out its uninteresting, impersonal, bland quality.

If you decide to use first-class mail you must be alert to every possibility for gaining efficiency and economy. For example, we can buy a mailing list and, for 32 cents apiece, send a brochure to every special education teacher in a four-county area. But we can cut our costs in half if we send two flyers in the same envelope, one stamped "special education teacher" and the second "Please share with an interested parent." We can cut the cost in half again if we address the envelope to the school principal and insert four flyers, one directed to the principal, the two mentioned above, and a fourth flyer stamped "Please Post." And because we can mail five single sheets of paper in a business envelope for the first-class rate, we might also enclose another that reads "School Psychologist." Or better yet, because we know that psychologists, nurses, and social workers travel from school to school, how about putting a flyer addressed to each of them in a third of the envelopes? Now our mailing costs are down to about seven cents per person, and we can reach 10,000 people for $700.

Using 3rd-class, or what is called bulk mail, is less expensive still, but you have to be careful. A lot of bulk mail is thrown away unread so we want to disguise our mail if we can. We do that by using 4th-class mail in a special way. Let's assume there are 100 school districts in a four-county area in which we want to promote a program for educators and interested parents. We plan on distributing 10,000 flyers using the five-in-one envelope strategy outlined earlier. Rather than put first-class postage on each envelope addressed to every principal, we will put all the envelopes for the principals in a particular school district into a larger Manila envelope and send that, using 4th-class mail rates, to the school district central office. With 10,000 flyers, five to an envelope, we have 2,000 envelopes. If there are 100 school districts in the four counties, we will need 100 large envelopes with, on the average, 20 smaller envelopes inserted in each. You can use what is called "special 4th-class" mail to send the large envelopes to the central school district office for a cost between $1.24 and $1.74 for a total of $124 to $174. The only sacrifice you make using this method is that there is more work to be done to prepare the mailing, and you have to mail about a week earlier to ensure that 4th-class mail delivery and the internal mail system of the school district have time to distribute your material. You can obtain guidance regarding mailing from the postmaster at your local post office or get a copy of the *United States Post Office Domestic Mail Manual* (1995), which is available at all post offices. Some types of mail, such as 3rd-class or bulk mail, have very strict requirements about uniformity of shape and weight, sorting, and other requirements that may make the process unwieldy.

But note our use of 4th-class mail in the previous example. The only people who see the large Manila envelopes are those who open them in the mail room or at a secretary's desk. The final consumer receives a crisp white envelope addressed to him or her, by name and title. There may be a place for 3rd-class bulk mail under other circumstances (i.e., if when you are delivering a glossy catalog of multiple seminars to an individual or institution to keep as a reference and the catalog is sufficiently attractive to overcome the shoddy image of bulk mail), but they are limited and distinct. Always consider the use of first-class mail if at all possible.

Delivering a brochure to a potential registrant represents a significant portion of the marketing budget, but that does not mean you have to spend a great deal of money. We will have more to say in Chapter 8 about costs and finances, but here we can note that we rarely mail 10,000 flyers. Half that many is usually enough for any of the programs described here. So if it costs about $25 per thousand to print flyers and postage costs only $200, it is easy to see that you can develop the skeleton of a large scale promotion with only a modest initial expenditure.

Marketing Brochure Checklist

Essential Elements

_____ 1. Name of the seminar

_____ 2. Who is sponsoring the seminar

_____ 3. Who is presenting the seminar

_____ 4. Seminar date(s)

_____ 5. Seminar location

_____ 6. Seminar start and stop times

_____ 7. Program description

_____ 8. Benefits to be gained from seminar

_____ 9. Registration instructions and form

_____ 10. Fee and payment information

_____ 11. Objectives/Outcomes from seminar

Useful Elements

_____ 1. Brief biography of seminar leaders

_____ 2. References/Testimonials from previous participants

_____ 3. Program schedule or agenda

_____ 4. Statement of who intended audience is

_____ 5. Seminar address and map

_____ 6. Telephone number and address of sponsoring organization

_____ 7. Information on refunds, substitutions, and walk-in registrations

_____ 8. Information on material included with the seminar

Useful Elements (Continued)

    ___   9. Statement that additional material will be available for purchase

    ___   10. Preprinted return address

    ___   11. How more information on the seminar may be obtained

    ___   12. Information about any CE credit offered

    ___   13. Discounts, guarantees, parking, and other administrative details

Other Considerations

    ___   1. Paper quality

    ___   2. Graphic art if indicated

    ___   3. Typeface

    ___   4. Style or fold of paper

    ___   5. Color

    ___   6. Layout

    ___   7. Drawings or photographs

    ___   8. Ink

    ___   9. Postal rates for different layouts

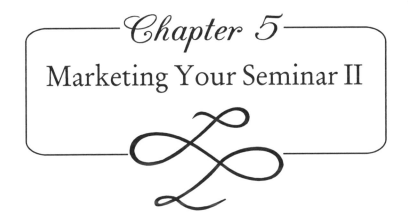

Chapter 5
Marketing Your Seminar II

There are many effective marketing strategies in addition to direct mail. Some are elaborate, highly structured, and expensive; others are relatively informal and inexpensive, such as announcing your seminar during the public service portion of a local radio station broadcast or delivering flyers, one at a time, to every house in your community, using the labor of your children and their friends. Among the most productive and least expensive marketing strategies are three alternatives: sponsored programs, co-sponsored programs, and in-house programs.

MARKETING THROUGH SPONSORED PROGRAMS

Many organizations are potential sponsors of your seminar. Your own clinic may want you to present a program to boost its profile in a competitive environment. Your hospital probably already has at least one lecture or seminar series and might be interested in including yours on their list. Local, state, and national professional organizations sponsor annual meetings, and, although most of their programs are relatively short and do not offer a fee, there are often longer workshops or seminars associated with these meetings that give you an opportunity to present your program and get paid for it.

Colleges and Universities

Many colleges and universities offer extensive continuing education programs, along with other courses of supplemental study that might accommodate your seminar. For example, most university continuing education programs offer seminars for psychologists, social workers, physicians, nurses, teachers, marriage counselors, and health care services administrators. Not only do continuing education departments need instructors for their own programs, they are usually open to suggestions for new programs from outsiders.

There are many ways to take advantage of the opportunities available through continuing education departments. For example, we have used them to test new seminars in order to keep our initial expenses low, but we have worked with them on programs that had already proven successful, too. Although some universities draw faculty for continuing education courses only from their own staff, most look beyond their own borders. Most of these departments are now self-funding. That is, they have to earn enough money to pay their own salaries and, they hope, make a little profit. There are usually minimal university appropriations to keep them afloat. So, more and more, we find well-trained business managers running these programs. They take seriously their responsibility to provide services to their graduates and others in their state, but many also realize that to survive, business has to come first. That means offering good programs that will attract large audiences. If you have something good to offer them, they will listen - and very often give it a try.

It is inexpensive to contact these departments directly, so we usually send a mailing every 6 months or so that consists of a cover letter, program outline, list of educational objectives, and a list of references. A sample letter appears on pages 121-122.

There are about 1,200 continuing education programs in colleges and universities in the United States. To reach them all using first-class postage costs about $400. We typically get 12 to 15 responses. Three or four of them will result in a sponsored program. We charge between $1,800 and $2,500 plus travel expenses for a full-day seminar, so you can see that a marketing effort of this type pays off readily. Six months later we send out another mailing and secure three or four more contracts. A year after our first mailing we will send another to the same schools we contacted the first time. We offer additional programs but also include information about the seminars discussed in earlier mailings. We get a good number of replies and inquiries from universities and colleges who had been on our earlier mailing list. We have sent our routine mailings to some schools a half-dozen times and only then have received a response that led to a workshop or seminar.

Once you have a system like this in place, it grows. Many of the continuing education departments invite us back year after year, or in some cases, every 6 months or so. A number of colleges organize programs all over the country. We have arrangements with several to present about a dozen programs a year in different parts of the country.

The 1-day seminar can often be extended into a short course lasting 2 or 3 days, which the university may offer for academic credit as part of its summer school program. For example, we have combined our AD/HD and Discipline Strategy seminars into a 3-day, 20-contact-hour program that fits neatly into the requirements most universities have for a one-credit course. We usually are able to schedule two or three of these each summer, when the rest of our seminar business is a bit slower. It provides a nice balance to the hectic pace of 1-day programs we present throughout most of the year.

Of course, these arrangements entail sacrifices as well as advantages. The chief advantage is that we have a guaranteed base of operations and income that requires no extra work on our part and, equally important, absolutely no investment of money. The university takes on all the responsibility. We just show up, do our job, and collect our fee. While the fee we are paid is usually less than our gross income for a similar workshop we organize and pay for ourselves, the net profit is similar because we do not have home office expenses, travel expenses, and meeting room and refreshments to pay for. In addition, having a few seminars built into the schedule of a hectic year that do not make demands on us for administration is a refreshing change.

Once you have one program scheduled with a continuing education department, it is easier to sell them to others. There is a national association of directors of college and university continuing education programs. As soon as you make one contact, you can ask for names at other universities. Now you can send letters with personal references that will open even more doors. But we started it all with "cold call" letters on a shoestring budget and now present about 30 days a year of university-related programs. This includes 2- and 3-day summer school courses which are expanded versions of several of our topics and other specialized programs.

There are still more opportunities within colleges and universities. Most professional schools offer continuing education for their graduates and other practicing professionals. So we have sold our seminars to continuing education departments in medical schools, nursing schools, schools of social work, departments of psychology, and colleges of education as well. Usually these organizations have an affiliation with the continuing education department, so contact with one of them leads to good contacts with many others.

Other departments and divisions of a university may also have continuing education programs, but we have not discussed them because they go beyond the topic of this book. These may be extensions of your work that would be applicable to departments of business, journalism, engineering, or others.

We will discuss setting fees and negotiating with continuing education departments when we discuss costs and other financial planning in Chapter 7. The institution usually has its own contract, so we just make sure our concerns are represented in the contract and do not insist on using our own. Contracts provided by most universities are far more complex than necessary, which probably reflects the usual bureaucratic morass you find in large institutions. If we have to provide a contract (and you should always have a written contract), we use a version of the Contract Letter on pages 123-124.

We have never had a very strict policy about cancellations of sponsored programs for one simple reason: it rarely happens. There has been only one occasion in 5 years when a sponsored program had to be canceled within 2 months of the program. So we think we build good will without worrying about protecting ourselves in legalistic language and threats against an occurrence that is so rare.

Small Sponsored Programs

Other colleges also offer adult education programs that may be especially helpful if you are at the beginning of your work in the seminar business, or even each time you develop a new program. You can get a quick and inexpensive test of the interest in your idea as well as get a captive audience to give you some feedback. These adult education programs usually consist of one to five "classes" of 60 to 90 minutes on topics ranging from home carpentry to updates on the current treatment of coronary artery disease or epilepsy. In fact, medical topics are especially popular. A benefit to offering a brief course is that you can get started with only a basic idea and a brief outline. You may have had several ideas for seminars that you are convinced will be popular, but the time needed for preliminary development work is more than you want to spend or can find in your busy schedule.

If you give the topic titles to the course directors at the local community college and high schools to add to their catalogs for the coming semester, you will get an idea of the interest in your topic. In fact, you won't even have to sit down and actually prepare the lecture until after you are sure enough people will register to make it worthwhile. And, unless, you happen to be among the handful of people who have the discipline to carry through on every project they initiate, this practice will provide the structure to get the job done. Of course, there is still a lot of work to be done after you complete even a very successful lecture, but if you are still interested in developing a full-scale seminar on the topic and marketing to a larger audience, you have a running start.

Seminar Companies

As you well know from the mail that crosses your desk each day, there are many companies that offer seminars to those in your profession as well as others in related fields. Several seminar companies are listed below. They might be interested in your idea. Like book publishers, seminar companies get a lot of submissions from people with ideas that are not very well worked out. Before contacting any of these companies, you should do your homework so you can offer a clear idea of what your seminar will be like. On the other hand, do not be surprised if they ask you to modify your program or expand a particular aspect of it. They may even say they are not interested, but they might ask if you are interested and capable of developing another idea that might reflect an angle on your original topic or one geared at a niche that you had not thought about.

Don't be put off by the fact that the seminar company may already have one or more seminars similar in content to what you have to offer. They will not want a duplicate, of course, but many companies do like to offer different, but related, seminars. They know that once you have convinced people you have a good product, you are more likely to sell them another seminar. It is always easier and less expensive to attract that person to a second seminar than it will be to acquire an entirely new customer.

Seminar Companies

American Healthcare Institute (AHI)
801 Wayne Avenue
Suite 200
Silver Springs, MD 20910
Telephone: 301-565-9200

Skillpath Seminars
P.O. Box 2768
Mission, KS 66201
Telephone: 800-873-7545

Padgett-Thompson
P.O. Box 8297
Overland Park, KS 66208
Telephone: 800-255-4141

Fred Pryor Seminars
2000 Johnson Drive
P.O. Box 2951
Shawnee Mission, KS 60201
Telephone: 800-255-6139

Speaker Bureaus

Speaker bureaus match speakers who have an interesting topic or entertaining presentation with organizations that need them. There is a top tier of speakers and agents who represent them. These speakers include ex-presidents, international business and political figures, and entertainers. It is unlikely that representatives of these agencies would be interested in your seminar or speech on how diet and exercise maintain self-esteem. However, groups interested in celebrity speakers are in the minority, and the encouraging fact is that your talk on self-esteem is likely to be more attractive to more people than Henry Kissinger's assessment of post cold-war Europe. Businesses, hospitals, public service agencies, schools, and professional associations all need speakers for meetings on local, state, and national levels. It does not cost you very much to call a few speaker bureaus to see if they are interested in what you have to offer. Inquiries of this type give you another opportunity to try out your ideas with people who make their living offering similar programs to the public. They can give you a lot of useful information even when they turn you down or suggest you modify your program and try again.

Speaker bureaus look for speakers who can deliver interesting talks to their clients, who may have very specific interests. If you are an endocrinologist who speaks about problems of noncompliance in diabetic patients, you will be a welcome speaker not only at a meeting of your colleagues but also at meetings of laypersons with diabetes. If you can extend your knowledge of issues related to medical compliance, you might also be able to address other audiences on medical compliance in other specialties or even related nonmedical areas.

But many times agents are instructed to locate an "interesting speaker" regardless of the topic. So if you can deliver a speech on recent developments in your line of work or profession in a way that makes it interesting for a general audience, especially if you are a good enough speaker to make the presentation entertaining, you may have a wide range of opportunities from which to choose. On the next page, we have included a list of speakers bureaus. Send them a brief, emphasis *brief,* description of your seminar or speech and see what they have to say.

Speakers Bureaus

Washington Speakers Bureau
1663 Prince Street
Alexandria, VA 22314
Telephone: 703-684-0555

Keppler Associates
4350 N. Fairfax Drive
Suite 700
Arlington, VA 22203
Telephone: 703-516-4000

Leading Authorities
919 18th Street NW
Suite 500
Washington, DC 20006
Telephone: 202-783-0300

MARKETING THROUGH CO-SPONSORS

Who are co-sponsors? Co-sponsors are agencies, organizations, or even individuals who will share the cost and effort of promoting a seminar with you. A co-sponsor is a partner, although the partnership is not always equal. Because we present a lot of programs on Attention-Deficit/Hyperactivity Disorder, we have often worked with community or parent support groups such as Children With Attention Deficit Disorder (CHADD) or the Attention Deficit Disorder Association (ADDA). Occasionally, these organizations will decide to accept the full responsibility for putting on a program and just hire us to present the program. That becomes a sponsored program. On other occasions, we find co-sponsors in a hospital or clinic. There are many ways to attract a co-sponsor. Our first co-sponsors were individuals from distant towns who attended our seminars. Using evaluation forms, or the spontaneous comments of some people who said, "This was a terrific program; I wish we had something like it in our town," we made contact with individuals or, more often a community group they belonged to, and we set up a co-sponsorship arrangement.

There are many advantages of having a co-sponsor, but two stand out. Sponsors share the work (although they usually share the profit, too), and having an association with a nonprofit co-sponsor opens a lot of doors for exceptionally modest cost. Materials, meeting sites, advertising, and labor are often very inexpensive. It is not unusual, if working with a co-sponsor, to have the meeting site donated. You will also have access to church auditoriums or schools that might be denied to you as a profit-making entity. Refreshments are donated by individuals who prepare them or local stores who are solicited by members of the groups, and it is all done without you. Usually, there is a printer or someone in the group with graphic design skills who can design flyers and other advertising. Newspapers and radio stations will run announcements for nonprofit organizations more readily, and at no charge, than for someone else who is in business. Usually the group has a mailing list already in place and a regular mailing that can include the announcement of your program. There is ample volunteer labor to address envelopes or make personal contacts. For example, when we did one program on depression and suicide in children, about a dozen parents volunteered to meet briefly at a staff meeting at each of 76 schools in the county to deliver publicity material and announce the program. They also delivered flyers to every pediatrician, general practitioner, and mental health clinic in a four-county area. Finally, if you are not especially well known in the community, the association with a local organization will add to your credibility.

If you are a health care professional and offer a seminar on a particular topic, say teen eating disorders or nursing care of the head-injured patient, and you have lived and practiced in your community for a few years, you will know people from your practice who are members of community groups that might be an appropriate co-sponsor. Most of these groups are interested in anything that will promote awareness and offer new information to their group and to the community at large, so it is not difficult to make the contact and set up the co-sponsorship arrangements. But even if you do not have the personal contacts, the organizations are accessible through the phone book. Call and explain what you are doing. This usually leads to enthusiastic cooperation. If you have done your homework well in the early stages of topic development, you may have some of these individuals on your advisory committee, or they might have completed one of your questionnaires so they are already familiar with what you are doing.

National and state organizations may be helpful, but the groups who will be most helpful are local, and you will have to track them down. Fortunately, it is easy. There are dozens of such groups, if not hundreds. On page 109, there is a partial list of different types of nonprofit groups taken from a single day's listing in a newspaper in our area.

This is only a small selection from a much longer list that is published once a week. It fills two pages with names of several hundred organizations, community services, voluntary associations, support groups, and others. They are easy to find, usually staffed by serious, committed people who, if you have something valuable to offer, will work hard on your behalf. Sometimes, even if you cannot establish a co-sponsor arrangement or if you are co-sponsored by another group, you will be able to insert your flyer or brochure into the routine mailing that other groups send to their members. Sometimes you can do it free. Other times you will find that a modest donation of $25 is a good idea, but you can do this with several groups and reach an audience that your other publicity might miss.

Other Co-Sponsors

General medical practices, mental health clinics, group practices, hospitals, and community service and social service agencies, such as Catholic Charities, Lutheran Family Services, or Jewish Family Services, are also potential co-sponsors. Private colleges or community colleges who have their own adult education or continuing education programs and have not been interested in hiring you to present one of their programs may still be interested in a co-sponsorship arrangement that will give you access to some of their resources and give them a chance to see what you have to offer.

TABLE 5-1: PARTIAL LIST OF POTENTIAL CO-SPONSOR GROUPS	
Adoption Issues	Gamblers Anonymous
Birth Parent Support Group	Early Menopause Group
Co-Dependents Anonymous	Women's Resource Center
Dyslexia Support Group	Domestic Violence Project
Mothers of Children With Neurological Disorders	Home Health Care
	Nurse-Midwife Services
Starting Over for Widowers and Widows	Children and Adults With AD/HD
Relatives of Aging Persons	Debtors Anonymous
Association for Children's Mental Health	Emotions Anonymous
	Black Parent Support Group
Head Injury Family Support Group	Pet Loss Support Group
	Low Vision Support Group
Smoke Stoppers	Aphasia Support Group
Child Care Network	Herpes Support Group
HIV/AIDS Resource Center	Diabetes Group
Ostomy Association	Family Counseling Service
Batterers Accountability	Arthritis Foundation
Care Givers Support Group	Children's Rights Group
Divorce After 60	

Use the exercise on pages 125-130 to come up with groups you might contact regarding co-sponsoring your program.

THE CUSTOM IN-HOUSE SEMINAR

There are institutions and businesses that can use your program for their staffs. This might be a seminar on a clinical topic for the staff of a hospital department, rehabilitation center, or mental health clinic. It could be a program on stress management for the workforce in a factory. With a little attention to the details and angle of the program, you can make the same material applicable to a broad array of settings. For example, we have sold our seminar on AD/HD to schools, school districts, and state associations such as the Learning Disability Association and Society of Clinical Psychologists. We presented a program on the diagnosis and management of children with depression to several state associations for social workers and varieties of the same program to school districts for their special services staff, who usually are comprised of school social workers, nurses, and psychologists.

In addition to selling your own seminar to hospitals, clinics, schools, and other organizations, you should familiarize yourself with the types of training programs and the topics that are of interest, not only to these familiar institutions, but to other businesses and industries in your community as well. You will find that many of the services these organizations routinely buy are ones you provide. In fact, an analysis of corporate budgets for staff training during the first 5 years of this decade by *Training Magazine* (1996) indicates that training programs, health programs, and interpersonal relationships and communication seminars and training taken together is a rapidly growing area, representing boom times for anyone providing these services.

Much of this training is industry specific or technical, but much also falls within the purview of health professionals. For example, the same survey of training budgets for the years 1990 to 1995 shows that 30% of all American industry and government agencies hire outside people to conduct training programs about substance abuse and nearly one-fourth of all institutions, public and private, have AIDS education programs which almost always include a substantial behavioral/psychological component. In addition, 60% of the companies surveyed offer stress management seminars, and 45% offer their employees smoking cessation programs. Over all, about half of these programs are provided by employees of the companies with the balance coming from outside contractors.

There are fads and hot topics in this realm as well. In 1996, the hottest new topic was diversity training, helping people with different backgrounds and experiences get along with each other better. The fads come and go, but the general trend in providing these programs to employees of corporations, public service and administration, health services, and all levels and types of industries and businesses is up, and that means more opportunities for seminars and workshops for those who want to pursue them. Initial contacts with representatives of these organizations should be part of your market research, and programs you develop should be tightly tied to what they request. But once your reputation is established, you should find a more receptive audience for proposals on topics of your own.

Marketing by Telephone

Very few people are comfortable making cold calls - that is, a call to someone they have never spoken to before and who has not expressed any interest in their seminar. But one nurse of our acquaintance who earns a substantial supplement to her income from offering seminars on topics that include wellness, nutrition, exercise, and stress management uses the phone very effectively. In fact, she advertises only by phone. She calls 100 people who have attended prior programs. She tells them what she is offering next and urges them to pass along the information. She has some flyers available if anyone asks for one, but she does no other mailing or phoning. It takes quite a bit of time to get through to 100 people and a lot of self-discipline because many times she gets an answering machine or there is no answer. After calling 60 or 70 people there is terrible temptation to say to herself, "Well, maybe that's enough this time," but she finds the inner strength to keep going. And it works.

Given the nature of her programs, she needs only 25 to 30 registrants for each program to make a reasonable profit. She usually gets that many or more from word-of-mouth advertising she initiates with her phone calls. Often, people she calls, who had attended previous seminars on different topics, register for the current one. This may not work for you. In fact, it probably would not work for a lot of people, but it is an excellent illustration of an alternative strategy that works in this particular niche.

Radio Advertising

We use very little radio advertising because, to be used effectively, it is quite expensive. In addition, radio advertising reaches a wide audience, only a small number of whom will have an interest in our programs. Use of radio marketing is often a good idea, however, when you want to reach large numbers of people from different demographic groups, so it can be used effectively for programs for the general public. The cost of radio ads varies greatly depending on the market in which the radio station broadcasts, the size of their listening audience, and the time of day you advertise. You should be able to purchase 30-second commercials on most radio stations for about $150 during their busiest times - the times when they have the largest listening audience. You will, however, have to repeat your advertisement many times for maximum effect, but there is usually a substantial discount when you do this.

Press Releases and Newspaper Advertising

A press release is easy to prepare and often attracts a lot of attention. You can write brief, practical, attention-getting press releases yourself with a little practice. We have included a sample press release on page 131. Many newspapers, especially weekly or small local papers, rely on press releases for a substantial portion of their material. They do not have enough reporters to seek out news, even that of local events, so you can usually be sure that your press release will receive a reading and, often, publication. There is a less formal way to get mentioned in the newspaper, too. Most newspapers run a weekly column announcing public interest events. You will certainly see your seminar listed if you have a co-sponsor that is nonprofit. But even if you do not, you should give it a try. Don't be intimated by the large urban daily newspapers. They publish the same columns. The disadvantage of this type of publicity is that the column usually runs the same week as your program, so readers do not get much advance notice.

We rarely buy newspaper ads because using newspaper ads effectively requires repeated exposure. A single ad of sufficient size to attract attention is expensive and will not, by itself, have the impact you might wish. You would need to run a series of ads which is almost always much too costly. Depending on the topic of your seminar, a newspaper ad, like a radio commercial, is also usually too broad in application. You may pay to bring your ad to the attention of several hundred thousand readers when only 1% or 2% are even potential audience members. But don't forget your co-sponsors. We struck a deal with one university where we publicized our half-day AD/HD program in our usual ways, while our co-sponsor, the university, was able to secure a free ad in the major local daily newspaper that reached 300,000 homes.

See if you can interest a newspaper in doing a feature story on your seminar topic. Most newspapers have weekly sections devoted to lifestyle, family relationships, medical topics, mental health, and others. At even the largest newspapers, there are only a few writers who are assigned these stories. Find out who writes about topics similar to yours and give the reporter a call. You won't be intruding. They are used to phone calls and often are grateful because they feel pressure to produce something interesting for their readers every few days. Explain who you are and what you do. Point out that there is so much interest in your topic that you are planning a seminar or workshop. Do not try to sell your seminar. The reporter will be fair to you and mention your seminar in the article if one is written but will not want to feel exploited. You will be interviewed, and the reporter will likely ask you for the names of others who can be interviewed. Give them freely. Don't be greedy. Your seminar will be mentioned, and you will be quoted in the article. Feature stories are usually written and run in the paper within a week to 10 days after your interview.

Offering Continuing Education Credit

Many professions require continuing education (CE) credit units for continuing licensure. The requirement may be part of state licensing or a requirement of a national professional organization. Most professions have at least informal CE requirements, and many, such as medicine, nursing, rehabilitation counseling, audiology, speech pathology, and in most states, psychology, have specific requirements that must be met. Because these professionals have to attend some CE programs, it is easier to sell them yours if they also get the CE credit they need. You must be approved by a licensing agency or professional organization to offer continuing education units. You will have to fill out an application form and describe your program. This is usually easy to do because the questions asked are the ones you have already addressed in early planning, such as "Who is your primary audience?" "What is the content of your program?" and "What are the educational objectives?" We usually just give registrants our own certificate for their records (see page 115).

The national offices of all professional organizations are listed in the *Encyclopedia of Associations* (Jaszczak, 1997). Here you will find the names, addresses, and phone numbers of these professional groups who can give you more information on offering CE credit. If you want to contact the state office of any organization, you can get that listing from the national office. Do not be intimidated by this task. Most applications are similar and, although filling out the first one will take you a few hours, after that it is a simple matter of routine, and the benefit for registration is significant. Approval usually covers all your seminars for 1 to 3 years. As an alternative, there are also several umbrella organizations in business to certify professional programs and save you the effort of making individual applications to all of them. A list of National Professional Organizations is presented on page 116. Some professional organizations and some state licensing departments will accept certificates of CE credit from these organizations, but some will not. You will have to make inquiries in your state with the professional groups you are interested in and make your own plans.

SAMPLE

Certificate of Attendance

This is to certify that _____ Jane Doe _____ has successfully completed the following Continuing Education Activity:

Management of Children and Adolescents With
Attention-Deficit/Hyperactivity Disorder
Name of Workshop

Ronald J. Friedman, PhD & Penny Altman, MA
Names of Presenters

5.5
CE Hours/Credits

Educational Development Center
26801 Huntington Road
Huntington Woods, MI   48070
Sponsoring Organization

July 15, 1997
Date

Should You Offer a Discount for Early Registration?

While this may seem more an administrative rather than a marketing issue, the only reason to even consider such a question is if you will sell your seminar to more people if you offer a

National Professional Organizations*

Accreditation Council for
  Continuing Medical Education
American Medical Association
515 N. State Street
Chicago, IL 60610
Telephone: 312-464-2500

American Mental Health
  Counselors Association
801 N. Fairfax
Alexandria, VA 22314
Telephone: 800-326-2642

American Nurses Association
600 Maryland Avenue SW
Washington, DC 20024
Telephone: 202-651-7000

American Occupational
  Therapy Association
4720 Montgomery Lane
Bethesda, MD 20824
Telephone: 301-652-2682

American Physical Therapy
  Association
1111 N. Fairfax Street
Alexandria, VA 22314
Telephone: 703-684-2782

American Psychiatric Association
1400 K Street NW
Washington, DC 20005
Telephone: 202-682-6000

American Psychological Association
750 First Street NE
Washington, DC 20002
Telephone: 202-336-5500

American Public Health
  Association
1015 15th Street NW
Washington, DC 20005
Telephone: 202-789-5600

American Speech and
  Hearing Association
10801 Rockville Pike
Rockville, MD 20852
Telephone: 301-897-5700

National Alliance of
  Nurse Practitioners
325 Pennsylvania Avenue SE
Washington, DC 20003
Telephone: 202-675-6350

National Association of
  School Nurses
P.O. Box 1300
Scarborough, ME 04070
Telephone: 207-883-2117

National Association of
  School Psychologists
4340 East-West Highway
Bethesda, MD 20814
Telephone: 301-657-0270

National Association of
  Social Workers
750 1st Street NW
Washington, DC 20002
Telephone: 202-408-8600

*If you prefer to apply to a state organization, the national office will be able to give you the address and phone number of affiliated state offices.

discount. Why else would you do it? So, it's marketing. We have always charged the same whether people register at the door or in advance. We see little advantage in offering a discount for advance registration. We know everyone likes a bargain, but the only question here is whether offering an advance registration discount increases your registration or creates some other economic advantage for you. For example, we rarely provide lunch for our audience, so we do not have to report head counts to hotels or caterers who often want to know a week or 2 in advance how many meals to prepare. They expect you to give them an accurate count and pay for unused meals or pay a premium for meals ordered at the last minute. In such a case we would have an economic incentive to encourage early registration so we could have a clear indication of number of meals to order.

Hotels always ask that you give them a count of the number of people you plan to have at your meeting at least 72 hours ahead of time. This applies only to functions that serve food, but they will ask for the number in other cases as well. Coffee or sweet rolls served during registration are another matter. The hotel can make adjustments to these items at the last minute. If you are not serving meals and as long as your meeting room is big enough to accommodate people who want to register, we think it is best to let people know they can register at the door with no penalty.

Should You Require Advanced Registration or Allow Registration at the Door?

We encourage advance registration but always keep registration open at the door. Many people make plans at the last minute, so we never suggest that it is too late to register. If we have a choice between a room that seats 150 and another that seats 200, we rent the larger room so we don't run out of space. If we end up with a smaller enrollment, say 75 people, we re-set the chairs into a more intimate group or ask the hotel to set up tables. Occasionally we will fill a large room and have to turn some people way. We try to avoid such an occurrence with advance planning. We want to fill every seat in the room if we can. There will always be people who will see an announcement that registration has to be sent in before a certain date, and if it is after that date, they will call anyway to see if there is room. We don't know what percentage of people will do that but we know there is a significant percentage who will also see that notice and think it is too late when, in fact, we have the room to accommodate them. So we never suggest there is an absolute cut-off date even as we encourage people to register as early as possible.

We encourage people to register at the door for other reasons, too. Sometimes our advertising does not permeate to all levels of an organization until the last minute, or word-of-mouth advertising may carry news about our seminar for weeks, but some people don't hear about it until late. If we are working with schools, as we often do, we may not have as much lead time for advertising as we might like. For example, when we offer seminars for educators in early October we get more registrations at the door simply because the time between the first week of September, when teachers return to school and read our brochure, and the first week of October does not allow for the full bureaucratic decision-making process that gives a teacher permission to attend, process all the paper work for the school district to provide a substitute teacher, pay for the seminar, and still get the money and registration papers to us early. We know we will have a lot of people walk in the first few programs in October (and February) carrying purchase orders or checks for their registration. Some will have called to make sure there is space available and some won't. We want to accommodate them all, if possible.

One reason some seminar promoters do not endorse our hearty enthusiasm for at-the-door registration arises from the idea that people who register and pay early are certain to attend while those who have wavering commitments often wake up on the day of the seminar and decide to stay home. Undoubtedly, there are people who do not attend, but if they had sent in their money, they might have attended. Still, we have done so well over the years with walk-in registration and hearing from people who tell us that they just heard about the program that we are reluctant to do anything to discourage them.

Our experience presenting sponsored programs, especially for universities, has strengthened this conviction. Most organizations have what seem to us fairly rigid and arbitrary rules that get in the way of maximum success. For example, almost every hospital and university we have worked with prints a deadline for registration on the registration form. When we have inquired about why this occurs, we have heard half-hearted explanations about how a registration deadline encourages early registration (although no one has ever told us why or shown us any data that proves it is so). Actually, when we make further inquiries, the story is always the same. The registration deadline exists for bureaucratic convenience. It allows clerical tasks such as preparing final registration lists or printing handouts to be completed. These are important features of the program and not to be slighted, but it is a case of the tail wagging the dog. The primary concern of the seminar promoter should be to get as many people as possible to register, and all administrative and clerical jobs should be secondary and in service of the primary goal. As we have worked with many of these departments we have been able to persuade them to put their procedures in proper perspective. Allowing registration at the door has been one thing we have promoted, and we have found that most administrators, when they see the benefits to be gained, have been enthusiastic supporters ever after.

More than 50% of the people who enroll in our programs have their registration paid by someone else, usually their employer, so there is little incentive for an individual to register early. Schools, hospitals, and other institutions send in registration forms and payment depending on how quickly their bureaucracy processes the paperwork, not on what discount is offered. In our experience, some bureaucracies follow through promptly, while others put it off until the last minute. We have seen no evidence ourselves or research by others showing that differential fees have an effect on registration. It appears to be another example of "common wisdom" that sounds good and looks good but has no substance when you take a careful look at it.

Should You Give a Discount for Multiple Registrations?

Our experience with discounts for multiple registration is similar to that just mentioned. A discount for multiple registrations is usually more trouble than it is worth, and we have never seen a shred of evidence that the practice results in a larger number of registrations. In addition, a discount may create resentment in those who pay full price, or it may fill the room but may not yield any greater income. Your own circumstances may make a different approach work better for you. We have had many suggestions for modifying registration fees. For example, we have been told we should offer a discount for the registration of a parent to attend a seminar with a teacher if the registration is sent in with the teacher's registration. For certain programs such as the AD/HD seminar or a program on learning problems, it sounds like a terrific idea. We will implement such a plan as soon as someone helps us figure out a fair and sensible way to do it. We do offer one discount: We charge about $20 less for the second registration when both parents attend one of our seminars dealing with children's problems.

Finally, determine what works best for you. You will likely present more than one seminar. If you are uncertain about the best marketing plans, make a few small changes each time you offer your seminar. Decide for yourself which advertising medium, flyer format, registration schedule, or price works best. There is an intangible element in any business that cannot be taught; it can only be learned by experience. In the meantime we have offered some guidelines. You will know what is the best way for you to work after you have presented several programs.

Sample Letter to
Colleges and Universities
[Print on Your Letterhead]

July 15, 1997

Dear Sir/Madam:

We have had an excellent response to our continuing education programs on Attention-Deficit/Hyperactivity Disorder (AD/HD), so I'm
writing to give you an update to see if you are interested in scheduling
a workshop/seminar as part of your continuing education program. We
have also had a terrific response to our 20-contact-hour summer school
course offered at several universities.

   In addition to AD/HD, surveys show the *#1 topic* teachers request
for continuing education is help with *practical strategies for discipline.*
Enclosed is a flyer describing our program designed to meet this need.

   We have had 200 to 250 people registered for the AD/HD workshop
in Illinois, Wisconsin, Minnesota, Connecticut, Kansas, Michigan, Mis-
souri, Mississippi, Arizona, Indiana, North Dakota, Kentucky, and
California.

   Enclosed is a list of references. Valerie Anderson set up our most
recent "for credit" summer school 3-day course. She is at Portland Oregon State University, Department of Continuing Education. Her toll-free
phone number is 800-322-8887, extension 4706.

   There is especially strong interest among teachers, psychologists,
nurses, social workers, child care workers, and parents. Schools are now
required by law to provide for the needs of children with Attention-
Deficit/Hyperactivity Disorder, and most school districts are eagerly
looking for help. And, of course, discipline problems continue to increase, too.

In addition, our system of flexible financing has allowed continuing studies departments to take a chance on a program with only a very modest financial outlay.

Let me know if you want any additional information about either the AD/HD or Strategies of Discipline programs. I would also be happy to send you a complimentary copy of our new book, *Management of Children and Adolescents With Attention-Deficit/Hyperactivity Disorder.*

Sincerely,

Ronald J. Friedman, PhD

Enclosures: Program Outline
             List of Educational Objectives
             List of References

Sample Contract Letter to Colleges and Universities
[Print on Your Letterhead]

July 15, 1997

Ms. Roberta Caldwell
Director, Continuing Studies Program
University of South Central New Jersey
University Station, NJ 07784

Dear Ms. Caldwell:

Ron Friedman and I are looking forward to presenting a program on Attention-Deficit/Hyperactivity Disorder at the University of South Central New Jersey on October 22, 1997. The program will run from 8:30 a.m. until 3:30 p.m. Enclosed are 12 pages of handout material we would like copied for each person in attendance.

As discussed, our fee for this program is $2,500. In addition, we ask to be reimbursed for all travel expenses, which will include round-trip airfare for the two of us, two nights in a local hotel, rental car, and appropriate meals. We will make our own travel arrangements and submit a list of expenses to you immediately following the program.

We will bring a supply of books and tapes we will offer for sale. Please arrange a display area for this material.

We understand you will need at least 35 registrants in order to ensure a successful program. If your enrollment is insufficient and you find you must cancel the program prior to 14 days before the date of the seminar, you will not owe us anything except reimbursement for any airplane tickets or other expenses we incurred at your direction that cannot be recovered in any other way.

If the terms set out in this letter are satisfactory, please sign one copy and return it to us within the next 10 days. Thank you.

Sincerely,

Penny Altman, MA

Enclosure: Handout Materials

****

I accept the terms described above.

Signature: _____

Title: _____

Date: _____

Exercise for Identifying Potential Workshop Co-Sponsors

Which of the following types of organizations are possible co-sponsors for your seminar? Stretch and be creative in your thinking. Check all that might apply and then complete the remaining information.

☐ 1. Universities/Colleges might be willing to co-sponsor my seminar because

 a. _____

 b. _____

 Two of the best universities/colleges for me to contact about co-sponsorship are

 (1.) _____

 (2.) _____

☐ 2. Hospitals might be willing to co-sponsor my seminar because

 a. _____

 b. _____

 Two of the best hospitals for me to contact about co-sponsorship are

 (1.) _____

 (2.) _____

❐   3.   Companies/Businesses might be willing to co-sponsor my seminar because

a. _____
b. _____

Two of the best companies/businesses for me to contact about co-sponsorship are

(1.) _____
(2.) _____

❐   4.   Public/Private schools might be willing to co-sponsor my seminar because

a. _____
b. _____

Two of the best public/private schools for me to contact about co-sponsorship are

(1.)_____
(2.) _____

❐   5.   Clinics might be willing to co-sponsor my seminar because

a. _____
b. _____

Two of the best clinics for me to contact about co-sponsorship are

(1.) _____
(2.) _____

❐   6. Churches/Synagogues might be willing to co-sponsor my seminar because

a. _____

b. _____

Two of the best churches/synagogues for me to contact about co-sponsorship are

(1.) _____

(2.) _____

❐   7. Social service organizations might be willing to co-sponsor my seminar because

a. _____

b. _____

Two of the best social service organizations for me to contact about co-sponsorship are

(1.) _____

(2.) _____

❐   8. Group practices might be willing to co-sponsor my seminar because

a. _____

b. _____

Two of the best group practices for me to contact about co-sponsorship are

(1.) _____

(2.) _____

❐   9.   Seminar companies might be willing to co-sponsor my seminar because

a. _____

b. _____

Two of the best seminar companies for me to contact about co-sponsorship are

(1.)_____

(2.) _____

❐   10.   Professional associations/conferences might be willing to co-sponsor my seminar because

a. _____

b. _____

Two of the best professional associations/conferences for me to contact about co-sponsorship are

(1.)_____

(2.) _____

❐ 11.   Continuing education departments of professional schools might be willing to co-sponsor my seminar because

a. _____

b. _____

Two of the best continuing education departments of professional schools for me to contact about co-sponsorship are

(1.) _____

(2.) _____

☐ 12. Fraternal organizations might be willing to co-sponsor my seminar because

    a. _____

    b. _____

Two of the best fraternal organizations for me to contact about co-sponsorship are

    (1.) _____

    (2.) _____

☐ 13. Libraries might be willing to co-sponsor my seminar because

    a. _____

    b. _____

Two of the best libraries for me to contact about co-sponsorship are

    (1.) _____

    (2.) _____

☐ 14. Video producers might be willing to co-sponsor my seminar because

    a. _____

    b. _____

Two of the best video producers for me to contact about co-sponsorship are

    (1.) _____

    (2.) _____

❏   15. Other _____ might be willing to co-sponsor my seminar because

a. _____

b. _____

Two of the best _____ for me to contact about co-sponsorship are

(1.) _____

(2.) _____

Sample Press Release

NEWS RELEASE
JULY 15, 1997

FOR IMMEDIATE RELEASE

**Former Business Editor Starts
Hilltop Public Relations**

The former editor of *Business Quarterly Magazine*, Dennis C. Hill, has established a public relations practice in Jefferson, Oregon. Mr. Hill will be handling media/public/community relations and other services for clients in Jefferson and the Northwest United States.

Hill, a resident of Jefferson for 2 years, attended Northern Arizona University and Arizona State University, studying courses in several major fields. He has been involved in various projects in Jefferson, including serving as Vice-President and Director of Public Relations for NOVA Technological Center, a 1,100-acre business park adjacent to the Consolidated Space Operations Center (CSOC). He went on to serve as Editor-in-Chief of *Business Quarterly*.

Hill began his career with the *Hudson Register-Star*, Hudson, NY, in 1973, and he has been involved with various publications ever since. His new firm, HILLTOP CO., is located at 1202 E. San Miguel, Suite #1, Jefferson, OR 80909. Their telephone number is 333-555-2876.

For Further Information, Contact: Dennis C. Hill
HILLTOP CO.
1202 E. San Miguel, #1
Jefferson, OR 80909
Telephone: 333-555-2876

Chapter 6

Setting Up Your Seminar and Other Administrative Concerns

CHOOSING A LOCATION FOR YOUR SEMINAR

Your goals in offering a seminar will influence where it is held. For example, you already know how far people will travel to get to your office, so if your primary interest is to attract patients or clients, your seminar should be located in a facility that is nearby. On the other hand, you might want to see if you can attract patients who would travel farther than usual once they meet you and see what you have to offer. In the latter case, you want to go to them initially, so your seminar should be outside your usual area of operation. You will have even wider choices of locations for seminars of general interest or programs designed for a professional audience.

A meeting for a professional audience can usually be scheduled anywhere, downtown or in the suburbs, as long as the location is convenient. We usually select a hotel near a major highway intersection. It should be easy to find and easy to drive to.

Most people will drive 30 minutes to a professional meeting, and many will travel an hour or more. In rural areas, people are used to traveling long distances for routine needs, so if we present a program in Des Moines, Iowa or Albuquerque, New Mexico, for instance, we promote the seminar across the entire state. In larger urban areas, we typically advertise seminars on AD/HD, stress management, child discipline strategies, and the seminar based on this book within a 50-mile radius. Lay audiences usually will not travel as far. Other factors also influence registration. You will be familiar with these patterns in your community. For example, in Minneapolis it is hard to attract a suburban audience to a hotel downtown. In Detroit, residents of southern suburbs usually won't travel to seminars in northern suburbs even though they do not have to stop in the city itself. It is as if the city serves as an impenetrable barrier for them. Chicago is too big to attract an audience from the northern suburbs to a meeting site on the south side, but Los Angeles, which covers an area greater than Chicago and has a terrible reputation for traffic jams, does not seem to generate these feelings of barriers.

If you are not familiar with a community and don't know about commuting patterns, a good resource is the meeting planner or catering department representative at the hotel you are considering for your meeting. Ask if they hold many meetings at their hotel. Ask what groups typically hold meetings there and what they can tell you about commuting patterns. Tell them who you hope to attract to your seminar and ask for advice. They will usually have enough information to help you make a decision. Write or call the Chamber of Commerce. They will tell you what types of meetings are held in certain places and be able to answer more specific questions about whether your meeting would be appropriately placed at a particular hotel.

Type of Facility

Once you have narrowed down the location, usually you will still have a number of facilities to choose from. Meeting sites can be public or private. They can also be large or small, formal or informal. How are you going to decide? Many decisions are easy to make because they depend upon whom you hope to attract to your program and the content of your presentation. The structure of your seminar will also influence your choice of a meeting site. A lecture to several hundred people will work in a large room that would never do for a discussion group of 20 or 25 people. Most of our meetings are held in hotels, but we have used church basements, school gymnasiums and libraries, community conference centers, and the waiting rooms of large clinics.

First, see what you can get free. If you are not going to charge a fee for your program or lecture, or if the charge is only a few dollars to help meet expenses, you should be able to secure a meeting room in a school, church, or other community facility for no cost. If you can coordinate your meeting with a nonprofit community group, then most of the same free or very low cost facilities should be available to you even if you charge a larger admission fee.

Hotels and Convention Facilities

Usually we rent a meeting room in a hotel or community-owned convention facility. Unless our meeting is very large, we choose hotels because people are used to meeting in hotels, and even large hotels are still more intimate than convention facilities. Most hotels have similar arrangements for meeting rooms. The number and size of the meeting rooms vary from those appropriate for meetings of a dozen people to ballrooms that will accommodate hundreds and sometimes even thousands. Shop until you find what you need. Consider how you are treated by the staff of the facility from the moment you make your first phone call or inquiry. They will be interacting with your audience in a number of different ways, and their behavior will reflect on you. There is no reason to think that they will treat your guests or customers any differently than they treated you. If they meet your standards, then you are in good hands. If you experience frustration setting up even preliminary parts of the meeting, that does not bode well for your later needs or for the treatment of members of your audience.

The cost of the room will depend on the size and location of the hotel. In large cities, you may find the cost of meeting rooms in the center of the city prohibitively expensive, but in most cases you will be able to find a room in a convenient hotel for several hundred dollars. Do not hesitate to ask for a rate better than the one first quoted. In fact, we suggest you routinely ask for a lower rate. The catering or sales agent almost always has the authority to come down in price. We get rooms for less than the initial price quoted at least half of the time. Add 25% to the cost quoted for room and food charges. Most hotels charge an 18% service charge and an additional 6% to 8% for sales tax. These items will appear on the contract but will not be mentioned when you inquire about the cost of room rental on the phone.

We used to inspect every hotel and meeting room prior to renting it, but that is not possible now with our heavy schedule of seminars. Fortunately, we have found it is not necessary. We know what we want and can determine whether the room meets our needs during a phone call. On a rare occasion we are disappointed by some element of the meeting room but never to the extent that our seminar is compromised or our audience is uncomfortable. In our experience, the sales staffs in hotels are honest. If we cannot inspect a hotel, we ask how old the building is and when it was remodeled or renovated or redecorated. We ask very direct questions, such as how well kept it is. More than once we have been told that we would be disappointed with a facility and hotel sales representatives have recommended another hotel. Along with information about what groups have used a hotel and who typically chooses other facilities in the area, we have the information we need to make a choice.

Meeting Room Details

The more direct and specific your questions, the more useful the answers will be. For example, we have learned to ask more than how many people can be seated in a room. We ask the dimensions of the room, determine if there are any unusual elements to the layout of the room, such as a permanent platform or intrusion for storage that diminishes the available square footage, and then calculate ourselves how many people the room will hold. We do this because we have been given so many different quotes on how many people will fit into a room that is, say, 60 by 90 feet, that we cannot trust the figure, so we use our own. We know we can set 200 chairs very comfortably in a room that measures 60 by 90 feet, but we have been told by some hotels that the room will accommodate only 150 people and others have told us it will seat 300. For our purposes we may need a room that will hold 200 and to cut registration off at 150 denies us substantial revenue. On the other hand, to squeeze 300 chairs into the room may not upset the hotel management or even the fire marshall, but it would be a stressful day for our guests and our staff.

We have learned to ask how many chairs the hotel has available. Even in the largest hotels, there is a finite number of chairs. A room may hold 250 people, but if the hotel owns only 200 chairs or has several other small meetings that day and owns only 250 chairs, it does not matter how big the room is. Make sure the hotel representative knows how many seats you must have. This is rarely a problem when dealt with directly, but if not mentioned, every once in a while you will be unpleasantly surprised.

Make sure the room is proportional. You can probably work comfortably in a square room or a rectangular room, as long as the rectangle is not especially long and narrow. A 3-to-1 or even 4-to-1 width-to-length ratio is satisfactory. If the ratio is larger than that, you run the risk of having some people, not only far away, but with the feeling that they are sitting at the far end of a tunnel. A mitigating factor is the height of the ceiling. With a high ceiling, people sitting in the back may be just as far from the speaker, but the claustrophobic feeling is absent and they tend to be more comfortable. It is usually best to set the podium or speakers' table in the middle of a wide room than at the end of a long one. As long as people can see you, hear you, and see the projection screen, you will find it far less tiring to project yourself to the back of a short wide room than a narrow long one. This is true even with an excellent sound system. You will also note that you are a lot closer to the most distant participants than you would be in a longer narrow room.

Ensure that the temperature in the room is easy to adjust. Is the thermostat in your meeting room dependent on a control in another part of the building? Because many hotel meeting rooms are subdivided sections of larger rooms, we always ensure that we have control of the temperature in our room and the thermostat is not in the hands of someone next door. If there is a central control, make sure you know who controls it and discuss in advance how to respond to your needs promptly. Meeting rooms quickly become stuffy, too hot, or too cold.

Is the audiovisual equipment you need available and appropriate to the size of the room? If a projection screen is small, no matter where the projector is positioned, the image on the screen will also be small. Can it be seen in the back of the room? Audiovisual equipment is available for rental through the hotel, and we have never encountered a hotel that could not give us what we needed as long as we asked in advance.

Is the room quiet? Hotels will not book a rock music festival on the other side of an air wall that is not completely soundproof, but make sure the hotel conference manager knows about your need for a quiet room and have this written into the contract. If you visit the hotel, check it yourself by playing a tape recorder or radio in the adjoining room. One time, a group of gospel singers was presenting a performance in the room adjacent to ours. There were no empty rooms we could move to. The sound barrier would have been adequate to separate two *meeting* rooms but did not serve to contain the music. Apologies from the management who waived the fee for our room were all that we could expect, but that did nothing to make up to our audience for the distraction of the music. In this case, the error occurred because, after we had booked our meeting, the salesperson who handled meetings and conventions left for another job and her replacement, someone new to the business, booked the gospel singers without checking the schedule book. There is no way to avoid this kind of problem, but it is extremely rare. Problems such as this are almost nonexistent if you do your planning well.

Very few of our meetings require registrants to stay overnight, so we put less effort into ensuring that sleeping rooms in the hotel are up to our standards. We usually stay in the seminar hotel ourselves, so, of course, we want a decent room, but our primary concern is for our guests. If members of your audience will be staying at the hotel, you should satisfy yourself that the facility is satisfactory. There have been several hotel-building booms over the past 30 years, so there are large numbers of hotels that now need redecorating or even major renovations. For obvious marketing reasons, hotels always begin renovations in the lobby and public meeting rooms. So inquire about the sleeping rooms, too. Years may pass between the time the lobby is redone and the rooms are upgraded.

You should be able to negotiate a special rate that is lower than what the hotel calls its "corporate rate" if your registrants will use more than 10 sleeping rooms. In addition, if you guarantee a certain number of overnight rooms, you should be able to get the meeting room or rooms at no cost. This is especially true if you are serving a meal. Every hotel has a standard policy about how they set its charges and what you can have free if you buy something else, so inquire about these arrangements because that is your starting point for bargaining. You can usually do better. Even if you are just renting a meeting room for a few hours, the price is usually negotiable.

Make sure there is sufficient parking. If parking is not free, you should be able to negotiate a special rate for your registrants. You usually do not have to discuss parking in your brochure unless there is something unusual about the arrangements. For example, we recently held a seminar in a lovely free-standing meeting facility that was not part of a hotel or convention complex. There was limited on-street parking and no parking lot attached to the facility. However, arrangements had been made with the owners of a large parking lot about 150 feet away to accommodate guests at no charge. In this case it was important to let people know where to park before they arrived for the meeting because they might not be able to figure it out and this would create a lot of frustration and delay if left until the morning of the seminar.

Coffee and Snacks

People who attend a seminar expect coffee and tea. It is up to you whether you want to offer anything else such as juice, soft drinks, sweet rolls, or muffins in the mornings or other snacks at other times during the day. When you order coffee, ask to pay by the gallon. If that option is not available, it is acceptable to pay by the urn or carafe. Ask how much is in the urn or carafe so you have an idea of how much you are paying by the gallon. Hotels differ markedly in what they charge for coffee. For example, we have paid as little as $8 for a gallon of coffee and as much as $35. But even the highest price is a lot cheaper than paying by the person. Some hotels will charge an exorbitant amount for coffee service per person, for example, $3.95 for an early morning coffee service and $2 per person for coffee at breaks. That is nearly $6 per person. If you have 100 people in your audience, with taxes and gratuity you can wind up paying $700 or $800 for a few cups of coffee. If you serve soft drinks or juice, ask to be charged on the basis of consumption. Many hotels will set out drinks for everyone even though they know that only about half of them will be consumed. Then they charge you for the entire amount. These are not regarded as shady practices by catering companies and hotels, so you have to be alert and ask that you be charged only for what you use.

Providing a full meal may be a good idea especially if you want to make time available to network or socialize. At least one meal is often provided if a program lasts more than a single day. But we only offer meals when we have a specific reason for doing so. We don't often hold our meetings in out-of-the-way places, but if there is nowhere for your participants to go for lunch and the meeting facility offers only catered meals and does not have a restaurant, obviously you are going to have to make provisions for people to eat.

Shipping Materials

We usually ship books and handout material to the hotel before our arrival. Hotels have systems to deal with this, but often one department does not know how another department handles such arrangements. Make sure you know whom to address your shipment and where it will be stored. Get the name of the person responsible and determine who to talk to if you call or arrive at the hotel at a time when the person you have worked with is not available. We have never lost a box shipped in advance, but we have waited many anxious hours while hotel personnel tried to track down our material only to find it in the most unexpected storage area with no one available who could remember how it got there.

Make sure your shipments are well marked with instructions for the hotel or other conference site. A simple label similar to the sample below affixed near the address label will do the job.

IMPORTANT INSTRUCTIONS

This box contains materials for the following meeting:

_____Career Changes for Nurses_____

Date of Meeting:_____4/12/97_____

Boxes must be available at 7:00 a.m. on day of meeting. If you have any questions, please contact us at address/phone below.

Penny Altman, MA - Ronald J. Friedman, PhD
26801 Huntington Road
Huntington Woods, MI 48070
Telephone: 810-542-0762

Sample Hotel Instruction Label
(Affix next to shipping label)

Seating and Room Set-Up

We use two styles of chair arrangements. Theater seating refers to chairs set out in rows. Classroom seating describes chairs set at tables that accommodate four to six people. We seat people only on one side of the table so half our audience will not have their backs to us or have to turn awkwardly to see us. The advantage of classroom seating is that participants have a place to rest their materials and pens and pencils, as well as cups of coffee. Classroom seating takes about three times as much room and is usually not necessary for meetings of less that 2 hours or if there is not a great deal that participants will have to write. We balance participants' comfort and convenience with our own practical needs. If a room seats 150 people theater style and 60 classroom style, you cut your income substantially by limiting seating with tables in the room. In addition, even though it is more convenient to have a table to write on, each row is at least 5 to 6 feet further away from you and the front of the room if you use tables. If you have more than 10 rows of tables, a substantial number of your registrants will feel isolated in the back of the room. If you plan to hold a full-day seminar or workshop that will involve a lot of small group discussion, you can group 6 to 10 people at round tables, but for most programs round tables are not helpful.

We usually use theater-style seating except for programs that will require especially heavy amounts of paperwork. What we sacrifice in convenience we make up for in being able to put larger numbers of people in the room and gain a greater intimacy with our audiences because we are closer to them. If you do not have a lot of experience in this business, we suggest you visit the meeting room when it is set up in both ways. Sit in different parts of the room and see how it feels to you. If the room is not set up, you can still move around into different positions and gain some insight into how your participants will view the program.

We send a copy of the Hotel Set-Up Requirements Sheet (see pp. 157-158) to the person responsible for our seminar at the hotel at the same time we return the written contract.

Handout Material

We always provide some handout material. Depending on the program, it will vary from a half-dozen loose sheets to a bound seminar notebook. Handout material is of two kinds. Some will be used during the program. Examples include an outline with space for members of the audience to write notes, a list of area restaurants for lunch, and exercises that will be part of individual or small group activities throughout the day. We always hand out all this material before the meeting starts unless it is strategically better to do so at the time of the exercise. The second type of handout material is that which supplements the seminar and is intended to be carried home and used or referred to at a future time.

OFFICE ADMINISTRATION

Whether you conduct your seminars to build your practice, earn money, or add variety to your life, you have to concern yourself with practical administrative details. You will need two main systems: a procedure to keep track of all elements of the registration process and an accounting system to record income and expenses for tax purposes as well as for your own business planning. Income includes money collected for registration fees as well as any income earned from back-of-the-room sales. Your accounting system need not be complex, but it should enable you to break down your expenses into component parts to determine where your costs lie so you can plan how to achieve greatest economy. All of this requires good recordkeeping; fortunately, there are good, but simple, ways to do so that will satisfy your own needs as well as those of your accountant.

To start with, you should have a separate bank account for your seminar business even if you do not think of this as a separate business yet. You need not open a commercial account which usually costs more in bank charges, but an account dedicated to the seminar program will save you a lot of accounting effort later on. It will be especially important in helping to determine whether you are making any money. So keep business expenses separate from either your professional expenses or household/personal expenses. If you like you can obtain a "d.b.a.," which stands for "doing business as," in any name you choose and register it with the county in which you live or work. You can put this name on your advertising and on your checks. The d.b.a.

helps keep the seminar business separate from other financial and personal records while, at the same time, providing a more formal identity, but it is not a necessity.

If possible, put the money you think you will need to get the seminar up and running into your business account; then pay all seminar expenses out of that account. If you are doing only one program, your accounting needs will be minimal, but you still have to keep track of everything. A small notebook and your check register will suffice. You will also need a ledger sheet to keep track of registrants and what they have paid. If you plan to offer more than a few seminars or are hoping to build this into a bigger business, you should use a comprehensive, but straightforward, computer accounting system such as *Quicken* (1994), which will keep track of all your income and expenses and print it all out at the end of the year in a form that will satisfy the most demanding accountant or tax examiner.

If you do not have sufficient money available immediately to fund all of your anticipated budget, that will be no problem as long as you keep track of how much money you put into your seminar account, carefully monitor expenses, and pay all of your bills out of the seminar account even if that means transferring money into the seminar account only to pay it right back out again with another check.

Payment Options

Most registrants will mail a check along with their registration form. Others will send money orders and, in some cases, institutions will send purchase orders. And some will register at the door. We accept personal checks the same as we would accept cash and do not ask for any additional identification or validation. We have never experienced any problem accepting personal checks for registration or purchase of material at the seminar. Occasionally, a check will be returned unpaid, but this is not common. When a check is returned we ask the person who wrote it to replace it with another check or money order and, with very rare exceptions, this is done promptly.

Purchase orders (POs) are requests for a product or service from a business or institution with a promise to pay upon receipt of a bill or invoice. A PO is as good as cash but requires the added effort of sending a bill. Many institutions insist on using purchase orders even for small purchases such as seminar registration fees, so we accept them. We try to discourage purchase orders by saying we will accept POs only for five or more registrations, but that request is often ignored so we accept them anyway. A purchase order means that you will have to send a bill and track the account, which adds one more administrative step and a slight addition in cost. No one will inquire in advance as to whether you accept purchase orders because most schools, clinics, hospitals, and other large institutions buy things using POs every day and, to them, you are just one more vendor.

Should You Accept Credit Cards?

If you have a professional practice or other business where you accept credit cards and keeping accounts separate is not too difficult, then, by all means, accept credit cards. In addition, if you want to offer the convenience of fax or phone registration for your seminars, you will probably want to use credit cards. You can bill people for a registration taken over the phone, but it is clumsy, time consuming, and very expensive. On the other hand, we know of many small- and even moderate-sized seminar operations who do not use credit cards. It remains an open question about whether the use of plastic or other electronic funds transfer systems increases your number of registrations. In our opinion, if there is an advantage, it is quite modest.

And there is a cost associated with doing credit card business. It will cost you about $500 to get started. You will have to buy appropriate equipment, and the credit card management company will charge you from 2% to 4% of gross sales depending on your volume. That is not a great deal of money, but why give it away if you do not have to? Extra consideration has to be given to the use of credit cards if you plan to sell a lot of merchandise at your seminar because you will want to take advantage of impulse buying and that goes easier with a credit card. A representative of your bank will be able to discuss this in more detail and explain the costs and procedures further.

The Registration Process

We use an extremely simple registration process. You can design one of your own that fits your work style better, but keep it simple. We have three goals for our registration process: maintain an accurate list of the people who have registered for a particular seminar, keep a master list of past registrants for future use if we want to send them announcements or brochures about future programs, and maintain the records in an understandable form so that they are intelligible to an accountant or IRS auditor should we be asked to document our income. When registrations are received, the name and address and any other pertinent information are entered in a ledger (today most people find it more convenient and efficient to keep a computer file with the list of registrants for each seminar, but if you would prefer a hand-written ledger, that is just as easy to do if you are offering only one or a few seminars). We acknowledge receipt of the registration with a postcard. A sample receipt/postcard appears on page 147.

The card serves several functions: The registrant does not have to call to ask whether we have received his or her registration, and the card serves as receipt and admission ticket the day of the workshop. All we have to do is collect the cards or stamp them and return them if the person wants the card back for his or her records. That is how we can register 200 people with only one member of our staff at the registration desk the morning of the seminar.

We keep no other records. Most computer programs will be able to sort your registration lists in any way you choose to evaluate your audience later on. If you keep track of profession or employer or zip code, you can look at different combinations of data to fine tune your next mailing. When we present a new program in a location we have not visited before, we plot the attendance on a map to see where members of our audience have come from. We can determine if all of our mailing was necessary or see if there are areas we should have directed our marketing.

EDUCATIONAL DEVELOPMENT CENTER
26801 Huntington Road
Huntington Woods, MI 48070

WORKSHOP ADMISSION TICKET

Please present this card for admission. This card confirms that you are registered for the __Attention-Deficit/Hyperactivity Disorder__ seminar, in __Houston, Texas__ on __October 11, 1997__ at __8:30 a.m. to 3:15 p.m.__

Amount Paid: ___$69.00___

If you need a receipt, this card will be validated and returned to you at the registration desk the day of the workshop.

Receipt #89

Sample Postcard Registration Receipt

If, for example, we mail brochures for a seminar in Phoenix to every pediatrician in Arizona, but the farthest anyone has traveled turns out to be 100 miles, we can save considerable expense advertising our next Phoenix program for pediatricians by limiting where we mail our promotional material.

When to Mail Brochures

We suggest you mail brochures so they will arrive 6 to 8 weeks before the date of your seminar. This is the best window, but we have had success mailing only 4 or 5 weeks early and have had good registration with 10 weeks lead time. Circumstances will influence the time you mail your brochures, so rigid rules are to be avoided. For example, we usually offer a full schedule of seminars for educators. The best time for them to attend is during October and November, except for the week surrounding Thanksgiving. We would like to use the last week or 2 of September to broaden this window, but we cannot get our material to teachers in time to make it work.

We plan so our brochures land on teachers' desks several days after school begins in September. We want to avoid the slush piles of memos and envelopes that greet teachers on their first day at school, but we have to put our promotional material into their hands early enough so they can register, or at least secure administrative approval, for the programs we offer in the first days of October. If we were to follow our own advice and give ourselves a full 6 weeks lead time, that would mean that we could not schedule a seminar until the 3rd week of October because most schools do not begin until after Labor Day. Fortunately, this has not been a problem. We find that our programs in early October are as well attended as programs later in the fall. We do find that we are not able to judge as accurately how many people will just show up and register at the door. Our answering service assures everyone that there is plenty of space and they can register at the door. We want to avoid a lot of registrations mailed at the last minute because they may not arrive at our office before the seminar, and that can cause a great deal of confusion. Any registrations lost because we did not push people to register early is more than compensated for by the large number of people who walk in and register the day of the program.

Most businesses, clinics, hospitals, and public institutions have internal schedules that must be taken into consideration when scheduling seminars and planning marketing campaigns. All organizations have internal rhythms. Schools just offer a more pointed example, with discrete starting days each fall and ending days each summer. Time off for vacations affects all teachers, and the schools close down. This is not the case for hospitals and most other large organizations although summer tends to be less attractive for most seminar topics. Many small medical practices and clinics schedule a disproportionate number of vacations in August, so that month is the worst of the year for seminars except for the 2 to 3 weeks that surround Christmas. In most institutions, fall is the best time for workshops and seminars for any group although, except for the few days associated with major holidays, we have done seminars on just about every day of the year.

Still, if you can do your first programs in the fall or sometime in February through April you will maximize the chances for your success, and you can spread into other parts of the year when you have the confidence that comes from early success. Just as we know there are some months that do not work well for school people, there are also months to avoid when dealing with businesses and public institutions. July and August are vacation months, and while certain seminars do well then - we often do 2- and 3-day programs for summer schools at universities - individual and in-house programs do not do well in the summer. Avoid May and June if teachers or other educators are your target audience. By the end of the school year they are usually looking toward the same escape for the summer that students are, and it is not likely that you will attract a good audience at this time.

How Many Brochures Should You Mail?

The answer is, as many as you can afford to mail. Use your judgment. Do you have any data that will help you decide the number to mail? If this is a new venture, you will need some general guidelines. When selling a program to a professional audience, it is easier to answer this question than when you have a general interest topic. You will be guided as well by the geography of the region. What area are you trying to cover? You may decide to mail to all the mental health workers within a 75-mile radius or all the speech pathologists in a six-county area. Can you afford it? What is your purpose for the seminar? You know your community. You have to test others. We have learned that programs we offer for educators in Hartford, Connecticut, attract people from the Connecticut River Valley which parallels the path of Interstate 91. We are more likely to get a response from someone living 10 miles from the Interstate but 80 miles from Hartford than we are from someone who lives only 50 miles from Hartford but who has no Interstate to drive. Marietta, Georgia, is a suburb on the northwest side of Atlanta. We advertised a program in a 100-mile radius around Atlanta but, given our experience in other cities, did not know if people would come from southeast Atlanta. Crossing a large city seems to be a barrier in some places. So we plotted attendance on the map and found that we had a turnout that was roughly symmetrical, a circle with a 75-mile radius. Apparently, the city of Atlanta is not perceived as a barrier to people who have to cross it to get to a seminar that looks like it will meet their needs.

You may have heard or read that a response rate of 1% to 2% is good for a direct mail advertising campaign. While that is true in many cases, the real issue is not the percent return you get, but cost and profit. If you can distribute 10,000 flyers for a very small cost, half of 1% response may yield a very good profit. If the response is small but the fee you charge is larger, you will manage with a smaller number. In other cases the variables will be different and your distribution costs will be a little higher, but the response rate much better. Generally, you want to reach as many people as possible, of course, and this is especially true if you are offering a new seminar or one where you have not yet tested the market.

You can see how variable response rates can be from the following illustration. We distributed 3,000 brochures for a program on AD/HD in Hawaii and got an audience of 250 for a better than 8% response rate. We distributed 18,000 brochures for a similar program in New Jersey to be held in three different cities and had slightly better than 800 total registrants for a 4.4% response rate. For a seminar in New Mexico, we distributed 6,000 flyers and had an audience of 108 for a 1.8% response rate. Sometimes market research is more expensive than a trial run of your seminar. Brochures are cheap to print. Postage is not. Try 1,000 or 2,000 brochures and see what you get.

On the Day of the Seminar

Because we present most of our programs in distant cities, we usually arrive at the meeting hotel the night before the seminar. We always track down any boxes we shipped ahead, look over the meeting room, and double check to determine how the meeting will be posted on the hotel bulletin board in the morning. It does us little good to have the announcement board in the lobby use our corporate name, which most people will not recognize even if they wrote a check to that name 3 months earlier. We want the topic of the meeting listed along with the meeting room location. Since you will probably present your first seminars close to home, plan to arrive at the hotel 2 hours early to make sure everything is in place. That is more than enough time if everything is set up and in place as it should be - which it usually is. But you will need every minute of that time if something needs to be attended to at the last minute.

The staff at most hotels will work hard to make your meeting a success since their livelihood depends on your success. Meetings and conferences provide a large portion of the income at many hotels. But always double check yourself. Your instructions may not have been as clear as you think, or something else may need a last minute adjustment.

On our flyers and brochures we indicate a registration period of 30 minutes before the program starts, but some people will arrive 45 minutes to an hour beforehand. We like to be ready, so no one is told to go away or sees us in the process of setting up. It is more professional that way. We set a registration table at the door to the meeting room in the hallway or foyer with several flyers taped or tacked to the tablecloth and wall. Handouts are set out on the table, and we are ready to go.

152 Chapter 6: Setting Up Your Seminar

We use the same simple registration system the day of the seminar as we use in our office. We seek to minimize paperwork and allow one person to register as many as 200 people within a half-hour on the morning of a seminar. About 90% of registrants come in with their postcard receipt. Our registrar stamps the postcard to validate it and renders it "used," and the person is directed to the table where handout material is set out.

But that's too easy for most people. Their model of a seminar includes an elaborate registration process. It seems that is the way it is done in every case where those people running the program do not have to worry about the bottom line. Most people expect to have to sign a roster, pick up a name tag, and find a few sheets of paper listing the administrative issues of the day. So they might linger at the registration desk with uncertain looks on their faces. After we direct them to the handouts, we tell them that coffee is available in the room and nod toward the door, and that lets them know the registration process is over. There are still some who express surprise and ask if there is anything else they should do, but most are content; in fact, most are pleased with the simplicity of the process.

How Can We Make It Right?

If anything characterizes our approach to the business side of our seminars, it is our commitment to meet our customers' expectations and make everything right for them. We are not immune to criticism. Some criticism is fair, a lot is not. Of course we make mistakes, but we strive always to remedy everything for members of our audience no matter who is at fault.

We arrived at a hotel recently only to find that a large corporation, headquartered in the city, had booked a room for a meeting and the hotel had given them the meeting room they had promised us. We had a contract, but we were given a different room that was adequate, but inferior. No one responded to our protests. So we held our meeting in the room they gave us. Among other disadvantages, the audience could not clearly see the screen where we projected slides and other transparencies. We worked around the problem as best we could and, though we did a good job, toward the end of the seminar several people interrupted to complain; then the whole audience agreed.

Our response, as it always is, was to ask, "What can we do to make it right?" We had explained the circumstances of the hotel at the outset of the day, but understanding the reason and feeling its effect were not the same thing. After several minutes of discussion there was a consensus that we would make it right by providing each participant with copies of all the material presented on the screen even though it would have to mailed to them - at some expense on our part - after the meeting.

Because the room was crowded, we took an extra break. The hotel offered additional drinks and snacks in the afternoon, and most of our audience went away satisfied. Even if they were frustrated, they knew we had made an effort to do right by them. It was not our fault, of course, but it was still our responsibility to our audience to make it right.

We also persuaded the hotel management that a few extra soft drinks and some cookies in the afternoon would not be enough to satisfy us. They offered a 50% reduction in the charge for the room; we suggested they waive the entire charge, and they did. And, of course, we are not going to use that hotel again although we had held meetings there a half-dozen times in the past with no problems.

In another case, a woman, who had told us several times throughout the day what a good learning experience our seminar was, complained at the end of the day that the certificate we gave her for continuing education credits was not in the proper form for her accrediting professional association. She was angry. She said she had been misled by our advertising. She was wrong. We had a written agreement with her accrediting association acknowledging that they would accept the certificate we offered. All she had to do was send it to them just as she would do with any other certificate, but when we told her that, she disagreed. So we asked her what it would take to make things right for her. She continued to complain about the form of the certificate. We said we understood and would do whatever she thought was necessary to satisfy her. Finally, she stopped complaining and said, "You really don't want to hear any of this, do you?"

The truth was, we did not. We were not prepared to argue with her. We acknowledged her upset. We apologized for what she perceived as our part in causing it and wanted to move to a solution, but she was angry and did not want to let it go. So, in a sense making it right for her meant that we had to listen to her voice her displeasure for another few minutes. When she settled down, we again asked what we could do to make her happy, all the while fully aware that she would get her professional credit and that she had told us that the day had been professionally valuable for her.

Finally, she said she wanted her registration fee back so we gave it to her. We realized after she was gone that she also kept the certificate, so she had a fulfilling professional day, continuing education credit, and her money back. Not a bad day for her. But we adhered to our standards and know we did the right thing for ourselves, too.

Taking Criticism

We discussed the evaluation of your seminar in Chapter 3, but there remains the question of how you respond to the personal elements of criticism. You will not be able to please everyone. Anyone who meets and works with the public knows that, but knowing it and not letting criticism get you down are entirely different matters. You will get a lot of useful constructive criticism but also criticism that will frustrate and anger you and possibly eat away at your self-confidence if you let it. We are always interested in what people have to say about our programs; we believe that is one of the reasons we do a good job. But you have to have a sensitive internal barometer to let you know when you are getting feedback that is off the mark or receiving some of the baseless complaining that is unavoidable and goes with the territory. Our experiences have been similar to those of others who run seminars. We get complaints about the size of the room, the quality of the sound system, the nature or shape or color of the handout material, the visual aids, and the quality of coffee the hotel serves. We have had complaints (on more than one occasion) about the color of the carpet or wallpaper. We have heard from those who want healthier snacks instead of donuts and sweet rolls and those who laugh at us for serving "rabbit food." We have heard from roughly equal numbers who think we devote too much time and too little time to questions from the audience. We have been praised by those who think we are wonderful for letting people in the audience have their say and making useful contributions and from others who have taken us to task for wasting time letting people babble about their narrow self-interests when the person really came to hear us - the experts.

As we have become more experienced, we have learned to stop asking people what they thought about the snacks served at break or the ease of access to the facility or the cleanliness of the bathrooms. It is not that these things are not important. Of course they are, and we make a significant effort to make sure that they are satisfactory. We know the majority of people will be satisfied because we have done our homework. We have also found that there is little to be gained by asking people to complain about something. You wind up with information that is not of any use. Unless your meeting room is especially hot or cold, you will often find that some people are putting on their jackets just as others are reaching for a file folder to use as a fan. The comfort of your guests is extremely important, but do not let your concerns blind you to the fact that in a large group you cannot please everyone about everything. Put your primary effort into the quality of the program.

None of this, however, should be taken to suggest that we are not especially concerned about whether we delivered to people what they expected. There are really only two questions we want answered: Did you get what you came for? And if you did not, what was our failing? If we failed to deliver, we want to know how we can fix things for the person who complained and make sure it does not happen again. On the other hand, there will be times when people have expectations that we simply cannot meet and never promised to meet. Out of 100 parents or teachers who attend one of our programs on AD/HD, for example, there will be one or two who came expecting that we knew some secrets that would somehow enable them to be relieved of their burden in teaching or caring for a child. So every once in a while we will hear from one of these people that we still have not told them what to do.

In fact, by surveying the others in the audience we know that we have told them a great deal to do. But there are two qualifications. Caring for or teaching a child with AD/HD is a long hard struggle and there are no simple answers. AD/HD is a chronic problem and we cannot fix anything; we can only compensate for a child's disorder, and that means we are going to be involved with compensatory strategies for a long time. That is hard for some people to understand and/or accept. Those who do not accept it are likely to be frustrated and disappointed with our seminar because we don't have quick cures. We take to heart the message to us contained within this type of criticism. We have to do a better job of helping people understand the chronic nature of the disorder and just what can be expected in terms of treatment, education, and behavior management. But we will not be able to meet needs that are really dreams. We cannot fulfill fantasies.

Be careful what you promise. People will expect you to live up to your promises.

EDUCATIONAL DEVELOPMENT CENTER
26801 Huntington Road
Huntington Woods, MI 48070
Telephone: 810-542-0762

Hotel Set-Up Requirements

Note: Please contact Penny Altman or Ronald Friedman at the phone number above for any additional information once contract is finalized

On-Site Contacts: Penny Altman and Ronald Friedman

Post as: AD/HD WORKSHOP

Room Arrangements:

_____ chairs theater style (will call 72 hours prior)

Room must be quiet with no loud or distracting programs audible from adjoining rooms

Podium with microphone

Small table for speaker supplies in front of room

One 6- or 8-foot table outside room with chair and wastebasket. This will be used for registration.

Three 6- or 8-foot tables in back of room, with chair and wastebasket. These will be used for displays.

**No audience chairs or other items in space near display tables

Overhead projector with screen

Time Requirements:

Have room set up by 7:00 a.m. with hotel contact present

Program times: Start/8:30 a.m. - Finish/3:30 p.m.

Service room during 11:45 a.m. - 1:00 p.m. lunch break

Food and Beverages:

Have coffee and decaf coffee by the gallon or urn in room by 8:00 a.m.

Have water station throughout the day

Have coffee refreshed before 10:00 a.m. break

Pull coffee at lunch-time cleanup

Soft drinks to be brought in at 2:00 p.m./based on consumption

Pull remaining soft drinks at 2:30 p.m. and prepare final bill (to be ready by 3:00 p.m.)

Note: The number of gallons of coffee we will start with will be called into sales office 72 hours prior to program. Banquet representative should check with on-site contact before refreshing coffee in a.m. and for number of soft drinks to be put out in p.m.

Sleeping Room:

We request a reservation for one king/no smoking room for the night prior to the program date in the name of Penny Altman. We request this room at your best rate which may *not* be your corporate rate. Please make this reservation immediately and call us with the rate and confirmation number. Thank you.

Chapter 7
Financial Planning

Keeping a tight rein on costs is the key to success in any business. But to manage costs effectively you have to know what they are, and in the seminar business costs can be deceptive. Some expenses are difficult to quantify, too. For example, to what extent will you contribute your own labor to designing and promoting your seminar? Should you calculate all that time at your hourly rate? Should you record the cost of your labor at the time it occurs, or should the cost be spread over the months or years your seminar will run? Even if this is your first seminar, it will require quite a bit of your time and energy, so it is a good idea to keep track separately of direct costs, which represent out-of-pocket expenses, cash you have to spend, and indirect costs (i.e., the time and effort you put into the development of your seminar).

TYPES OF COSTS

Costs may be grouped into three categories: (a) development costs, (b) marketing/advertising costs, and (c) operating expenses.

Development costs are those associated with planning and getting your project off the ground. They include market analysis, need assessment, time spent writing and researching, test marketing, and anything else related to putting the seminar together. Marketing and advertising costs are pretty much self-explanatory, but it should be noted that there are often indirect costs involved, especially your time or the time of someone in your office that is needed to conduct surveys, call the printer for quotes on brochures, or make trips to the post office to buy stamps. Finally, operating costs refer to expenses incurred presenting the program. What does it cost to travel to the seminar site? How much does the hotel charge for the meeting room and the coffee break? What are the wages for people who handle registration? How much money could you have made if you had stayed in the office today and seen patients and billed for your time?

Direct costs are fairly easy to track, but indirect costs, while not impossible to track, are often either obscure or so much a part of your normal routine that you do not recognize them as costs until later. Then it may be difficult to recapture them and get an accurate picture of what you are paying to conduct a seminar. Whether you classify your own time as a direct or indirect cost depends on whether you have taken time that you would otherwise devote to earning income or used as leisure or discretionary time. Both types of costs should be accounted for. You will have a more realistic basis, not just for accounting, but also for making personal decisions. You can make better decisions about how much effort you are prepared to invest and what sacrifices you will make if you keep cost issues as clear as possible.

All of these decisions depend on how you view your seminar business. You must contribute some "sweat equity" to the development of any new business, but if you constantly think about how much of your own time you are spending, you may be discouraged from going ahead with the project. On the other hand, if every hour you put in on the seminar takes an hour away from your business or practice, an hour you would otherwise be paid for, then it would be foolhardy to ignore the financial commitment you are making.

For most of us, reality is a combination of many factors. We must sacrifice time in the early stages to get the project done. This is the time you take to read this book, for instance, or the time to attend our seminar. But most people find this time in their leisure or discretionary time, and it does not cost them much in actual loss of income. Still, not everything can be done in the evening. Consultation with mailing list brokers, printers, and even trips to the office supply store usually come out of the working day. And if you are diligent enough to get your seminar designed and ready to present, you will have to take some time from your regular work to present it, too. You will have to commit a substantial amount of your own time to the development of a seminar if you want it to be a success. There are many ways to economize in terms of the dollars you have to spend, but there is no substitute for hard work.

Development Costs

Everything you spend, including your own time, to research or create your seminar is a development cost. Not every dollar of development cost winds up in your project. You may spend money buying books that lead you into blind alleys or waste time searching the Internet for references that turn out to be useless. But most of your early expenses are either those that contribute to your own education and further understanding of your topic - and the topics of the competition because that is part of development costs, too - or expenses that are incurred for direct work on your seminar.

Development costs include many that are obvious and some not so obvious. If you do most of the work yourself, there will be few direct development expenses. Most expenses here are indirect and reflect your investment of time. In fact, project development can often be accomplished with only a few dollars spent to copy materials or books and journals.

These are examples of basic development costs:

- Books
- Journals and other literature
- Advisory committee expenses
- Questionnaire and survey expenses
- Paper and copying expenses
- Postage
- Salary for someone to collate surveys
- Salary for someone to make telephone surveys

Marketing/Advertising Costs

We will use our experience marketing a new seminar on Attention-Deficit/Hyperactivity Disorder to illustrate marketing and advertising costs. We have already used this seminar for illustrations earlier in the book and return to it now because it was the first seminar we developed with an eye toward a national market. We think that taking you through the development process, as we learned it, will be most instructive. In addition, we have presented nearly 600 of these programs in one form or another, so we have additional experience about how one idea leads to two and two lead to four, and so on.

The initial reason for offering the seminar was to attract attention to our clinical psychology practice. We also wanted to see if seminars might be a way to earn extra income. Seminars were also appealing because they were so different from what we did in the office. The variety and change of pace was a siren song. But just as hopes for extra income served to motivate us to start, concern about cost caused us to hesitate. It took a while to realize that if we could limit costs to a few hundred dollars, we were bound to attract a few people to our seminar. While we might not be fully reimbursed for our time, at least there would be some recovery of the money we spent for printing, postage, and a meeting room. When we finished our calculations, we realized that, at most, we could lose no more than a few hundred dollars.

It was an affordable risk for us. There are many times to move boldly, but spending money before you are sure you have a viable product is not one of them.

Typical direct costs are

- Brochure design
- Brochure printing
- Mailing lists
- General office supplies, such as envelopes, rubber stamps, and so forth
- Answering service
- Salary for person who sends out mail
- Salary for person who keeps track of money and client registration
- Postage
- Ownership or access to wordprocessing equipment
- Ownership or access to photocopying equipment
- Fees for photocopying any copyrighted material you want to hand out
- Fees to professional associations for offering CEU credit

We presented our first AD/HD seminar in 1988. Some expenses are greater now, but we want to show how we did it the first time when we were acutely aware of the cost and tried everything we could think of to keep costs down. We designed our own brochure. We showed it to a few people and asked the printer to give us an idea about layout, but the only expense was $15 for typesetting. In 1997 you can still get the same typesetting done at a quick print shop for less than $30.

We used a single sheet of colored paper, printed on both sides as shown on pages 84-85. We printed 5,000 copies. It cost about $30 per thousand for a total of $150. There is so much competition now in the printing business that in 1997 we can get the same printing order for $25 per thousand for a total of $125. To give you an idea of how a simple matter such as paper choice can contribute to cost, here is an illustration of different types of paper and printing we considered for a new program we recently developed:

Paper Costs for 5,000 Flyers Printed on Two Sides of Colored Paper

Standard paper stock we usually use	8½ x 11	$29 per 1,000
" " " " " "	8½ x 14	$51 per 1,000

(The big price jump is caused by the fact that the printer can print two of the smaller flyers at a time because of the size of paper purchased from the paper mill, but only one of the larger ones.)

Better quality paper	8½ x 11	$33 per 1,000
" " "	8½ x 14	$57 per 1,000
Coated paper	8½ x 11	$60 per 1,000
Adding a second color ink would cost an additional $20 per 1,000		

The cheapest lot of 5,000 flyers would cost $145, the most expensive $400, nearly three times as much. The same lesson can be learned at every step of the process. Of course, there are times you will choose the more expensive option because it is essential to your goal. But most of the time you can get exactly what you need inexpensively with no meaningful sacrifice.

In 1997, #10 standard business envelopes are available from any large office supply company for no more than $11 per thousand. One hundred 9" x 12" Manila envelopes will cost approximately $10. Add another $20 for several rubber stamps made to order, including one that has your return address on it. That's it for supplies to get started.

Let's track our expenses now. Our first market was educators. We phoned the state department of education in our state as well as local county and city school districts. Almost all had directories of personnel available at no charge. We have since learned it is a lot easier to buy these directories from a mail order company as we mentioned in Chapter 4. We spent our own time setting up the first program because we wanted to try everything ourselves and get the feel of it. We were willing to put in the hours because we were reluctant to put in the dollars. Using the procedure we described in Chapter 4, we addressed a flyer, with name only, to every special education teacher, school psychologist, nurse, counselor, principal, social worker, audiologist, speech pathologist, and physical therapist in every school in a three-county area. We also wrote "Please Post" on another flyer. These, in turn, all went into a white business envelope, and on the envelope we wrote the name of the school. These envelopes, in their turn, went into Manila envelopes that were mailed to the school district using the special 4th-class rate, usually for less than a dollar. In this particular three-county area of southeastern Michigan, there are about 80 school districts. Several were large and needed more than one Manila envelope. All together we wound up mailing about 110 envelopes at a cost of about 60 cents each for a total of $66. In 1997, with current postage rates, the same mailing would cost about $130.

We also mailed about 300 business-sized envelopes with five flyers inside using first-class mail. These went to schools in small districts where it did not make sense to mail a larger envelope, to private and religious schools, and to clinics, social service agencies, and other groups in the city we thought might have people who would be interested in our programs. This cost about $65. Finally, we sent 10 large packages of flyers to community groups such as the Learning Disabilities Association and support groups for children with Attention-Deficit/Hyperactivity Disorder. This cost an additional $10. Total postage cost was $140. The total cost to get the program up and running to this point, was a little over $300. In 1997 it would be prudent to double the cost of postage, but the other costs, as we noted, would be roughly the same, so the total for the same operation would be about $450, still a very modest amount to invest considering the potential pay off. We were charging a registration fee of $20 so we needed 15 registrants to break even at this point, but we now had to consider what we would have to pay to the hotel after the meeting for use of their facilities and the coffee we would serve. This brings us to operating expenses.

Operating Expenses

Operating expenses are costs you incur conducting your seminar. Many expenses seem to blend together, but for planning as well as monitoring, budgeting, and keeping as tight control as possible, it is best to view these different types of expenses as distinctly as you can. Operating expenses are a little more difficult to list because they vary more than other expenses. Not all operating expenses occur the day of the seminar. Many, such as answering services and processing of registrations, go on for weeks in advance and sometimes all year.

Typical operating expenses include

- Rental of meeting room space
- Audiovisual equipment rented from hotel or purchased
- Preparation of slides, handouts, and overhead illustrations
- Office supplies
- Salary for registrar on site and other helpers if needed
- Answering service
- Coffee or refreshments served to registrants
- Certificates of attendance for registrants (for some types of programs)
- Handout material

We reserved a meeting room in a nice hotel in a central location for which we paid $225. In 1996 we presented 94 seminars and paid $225 or less for over 55% of the meeting rooms. A few cost more, a few quite a bit more, but we have never paid over $500 for a meeting room and rarely over $400. At our first seminar, coffee wound up costing us quite a bit because we had a lot of people register, but let's wait a moment to tell about that. Add the hotel to our other up-front expenses and we were at $525. Now we needed 27 registrants to break even, but we would not have to pay the hotel until the seminar was over.

Keep in mind all the effort that had been expended and many small expenses. For example, we used our clinic address and phone number on the brochure so our office staff had to field phone calls and questions. Their time cost money. We now use a single answering service for all of our workshops across the country. They have enough knowledge of our operation so they can answer 95% of the calls. What they cannot answer they relay to our central office and we respond.

We addressed the envelopes, went to the post office to buy postage, took the mail to the mail box, all without direct expense but also all without any assistance. If you are not prepared to do this yourself, you will, of course, have to pay for it. That will add a fair amount to your cost but not a prohibitive amount.

You may be interested in knowing what sort of response we got to our mailing of about 4,500 brochures in the three-county urban area that includes the city of Detroit and all its suburbs. We received 297 registrations that first time in 1988 for a gross income of just about $6,000. We had to buy everyone a cup of coffee, of course, and that cost about a dollar apiece, so that added another $300 to expenses for coffee. (We have since learned there are cheaper ways to buy coffee.) On top of that we had two people from our office manage the registration desk and paid each of them $50 for the morning. Grand total of expenses including tips for hotel personnel who helped us was $975.

Were we well paid? That depends on how you assess the cost. It would not be an exaggeration to say that two of us put a total of 100 hours into development and administration. If our gross profit after direct expenses was $5,250, we were paid $52.50 an hour. Not bad, we think. If you keep in mind that much of the time spent developing this program was now past and that we could do it again for perhaps 25 hours of administrative time, the figures look better yet.

So we did. And we had another audience of about 300 people.

By the third time, we were ready to take a chance and spend a few extra dollars up front to relieve ourselves of the burden of addressing envelopes and licking stamps. That ran our costs up several hundred dollars, but we were no longer fearful that we would be stuck holding the bag. A little over 200 people attended our third seminar.

We have learned a lot and changed many of the details of our operation since then, but the core of our seminar business is built on what we learned the first few times we presented that program on AD/HD. We have streamlined or modified considerably. We have learned some tricks like this one to nearly double the bang we get for our advertising buck. In larger urban areas, or in states with two major population centers within 150 miles or so of each other, we prepare a brochure that lists two programs, one in each city, and mail it to people in overlapping areas so that many who live between the two cities get a flyer announcing two different dates in two different cities. For only about 20% additional in brochure and postage costs, we can advertise two programs. And sometimes we can do three in the same way - or four or five.

But whatever the refinements have been, the lessons we learned looking for effective but economical ways to get the job done have been our guiding principles.

When you compare the bare-bones budget from 1988 with one for 1997, there is very little difference.

	1988 cost	1997 cost
Brochure design	$ 20.00	$ 25.00
Printing	150.00	150.00
Office supplies	40.00	50.00
Postage	140.00	300.00
Meeting room	225.00	225.00
Salaries for registrars	100.00	150.00
Coffee break	300.00	75.00*
TOTAL	$975.00	$975.00

*We learned that hotels like to sell coffee based on numbers registered - that is, $2.50 per person. They know that only about 45% will actually drink coffee, so their profit is immense. But hotels will also sell coffee by the gallon or urn (ask how much is in the urn and calculate the per-gallon cost). Purchased by the gallon, coffee will cost 65% to 75% less than by other methods.

Figure 7-1: A Bare-Bones Budget for
Getting a Seminar Up and Running

We probably charged too little for that first program in 1988. We asked everyone to fill out an evaluation form, and one of the most frequent comments was along the line of "This was the best $20 I ever spent on a workshop or seminar." That pleased us immensely, of course, but when so many people say the same thing, it made us realize we should have charged more. We did raise the fee to $25 for the second program and kept it there for about another year before increasing it again.

You may not want to sell your program to schools, of course, but there are analogous ways to distribute your brochures and flyers to other institutions, such as mental health clinics, government agencies, and hospitals. Private practitioners in medicine, mental health, and social services are also easy to reach.

We have shown that you can get started in the seminar business for a modest cash outlay. We did it a few years ago; you can do it today. We now put more money into development and marketing in selected cases. We have more confidence in our judgment and the procedures we have developed over the years. We tend to view many of our expenditures as investments rather than gambles, but we are still careful. In the seminar business, as in most areas of human endeavor, you can solve problems a lot more effectively and efficiently with careful thought and planning than by throwing money at it. Albert Einstein is reported to have said that in any human endeavor, science or anything else, the proper formula is to spend 85% of your effort on planning and preparation and 15% on the action itself. Dispute the relative proportions if you like, but the principle remains a part of the rock-solid foundation of our approach to the seminar business.

One seminar we invested in more heavily than usual is the one based on the content of this book. We hired a design consultant to prepare a larger brochure, and we used several colors to print instead of just one. We selected paper stock for the brochures that was quite a bit better than what we used for some of our programs of more general interest. In addition, we presented the first few programs in large metropolitan areas where we knew there was the greatest concentration of possible registrants who would not have to pay to travel out of town or be away overnight. For every program we mailed 6,000 to 8,000 brochures to individuals and clinics using first-class mail. Our initial goal was to assess whether this workshop would attract an audience. We certainly want to attract that audience in the least expensive way possible, but if we confounded too many variables in our first few tests, we would not know where our success or failure came from.

We kept the price low, about half what we hoped ultimately to charge. We did not know the right price and because there was almost no competition in this area, we were unable to compare our price with anyone else's. But we did not want a high price to discourage attendance. What if we had a very interesting program that generated a lot of interest, but we had just priced it 50% too high so our attendance was so low we never got a good reading on the level of interest in the content of the program?

We conducted several trial runs to work out the rough spots and get focus group feedback. We charged no registration fee for the focus groups. In fact, we bought lunch for the people who attended. Then we took the program out of town for a trial.

Seminars Presented Out of Town

With an eye toward keeping costs to a minimum, we assume most people will want to present their first seminar close to home. At first, when we were new to the seminar business and went out of town, we ventured to cities no more than 150 miles away with our first programs on AD/HD. It is no more difficult to set up a seminar 1,000 miles away than across the street, but at first it seems harder, and it is more expensive. Also, because you will probably be less familiar with the market, it will be riskier. We tend to be more conservative and cautious than many others, but we have never regretted our caution. Typical expenses for an out-of-town program are presented in Figure 7-2 on page 171.

The average charge in 1994 for a full-day program for mental health and educator audiences was $70. It was about 50% higher for programs for physicians, but about the same $70 fee for other allied health professionals. At $70, based on the budget for an out-of-town seminar, 37 registrations would be needed to break even. In 1994 we presented 78 programs on AD/HD and 27 seminars on other topics. On three occasions, we did not get enough registrations to break even although our average attendance at all 105 programs was 118. We could have saved some effort

Print 6,000 brochures	$ 150.00
Postage to mail brochures	300.00
Salary for mailer	150.00
Office supplies	50.00
Answering service	25.00
Salary for registrar-advance registration	150.00
Telephone	50.00
Print handouts	50.00
Hotel meeting room	225.00
Coffee break	150.00
Airfare (for two)	550.00
Rental car	100.00
Hotel (2 nights)	150.00
Meals	150.00
Rent overhead projector, screen, and lavalier microphone	75.00
TOTAL	
	$2,325.00

Figure 7-2: Budget for an Out-of-Town Seminar

by canceling the programs with low attendance, but we presented them anyway. The main reason was cost. If we had, say, 30 people registered and went ahead with the program, our loss was modest. Even if we canceled the program and avoided airfare and hotel meeting room expenses, we still had nearly $1,000 already invested in the program, which was more than we would lose going ahead with it. But there is more to our decision than financial considerations. We do not like to cancel a seminar. Of course, we are in business and we have to make a profit, but we are professionals first and if we make a commitment, we follow through with it. We have yet to cancel a program because of low attendance.

We are fortunate because the law of averages takes care of us. Year after year we have seen that, while we may not be able to predict which cities or states will yield huge audiences and a generous profit, nonetheless, we know, on average, we can expect a certain amount for each seminar we present. We keep our costs in line, remain alert for greater efficiencies, and keep on going.

Why do some proven programs fail in some locations? Why are some cities or states better for some programs than for others? We don't know. Sometimes we make a guess or gather data that offer hints or hypotheses. But guessing and extrapolating from limited data is a dangerous business that can lead to serious and expensive errors. To add to the mystery, on occasion, we can have a hugely successful program such as we had in Columbia, South Carolina one Saturday morning a few years ago with about 200 people in attendance, only to return 6 months later and get an audience of 45. We had good feedback on a tried-and-true program. We talked to a number of participants who assured us that we were on track with the material we presented and met the needs and offered the benefits they expected, so we were confident that, while our effort may not have been perfect, we certainly did not alienate anyone and we would get plenty of good word of mouth. Our price was right, too. In addition, there had been no other program within several months that might have drained our pool of registrants. The community and surrounding area was big enough so that we were certain we had not exhausted our potential audience. So where were they the second time?

We didn't know, but because we had no reason to think it was anything other than a fluke and because we had done so well the first time, we scheduled a third program, this one at almost exactly the same time of year as the first one that had been so successful. This time 38 people registered. We have not been back to Columbia, South Carolina, with that program since, although we have had success with different seminars there. We still don't know what happened to change the response so dramatically. It is impossible to understand the motivation or lack of motivation of people who do not attend a seminar. You cannot ask them.

Sometimes answers are obvious. A hospital, university, or clinic may have conducted a seminar very much like yours the day before, but even the obvious answers usually do not tell the whole story. In most cities there is a large enough pool of potential registrants for many topics, so if the competition has November

10th sewn up, you can present your seminar on November 20th and get a good turnout. We have stopped trying to check each city to see what competitive programs might be running at a time similar to ours because we now offer 125 programs, usually on a dozen or more topics, each year, and it would be impossible to schedule them only when we were sure there was no competition. Besides, we think we are the competition to beat, so let the others worry about us. We have also discontinued most of our after-the-fact surveys that tried to assess why a program might have attracted only a small number as, say, in our example of South Carolina. The data we obtained, even when we used sophisticated and expensive sampling techniques, never gave us the kind of information that we could use in a practical way the next time.

Our programs on Attention-Deficit/Hyperactivity Disorder have provided our largest amount of experience. We present 75 to 80 AD/HD seminars a year across the country. AD/HD has become a very popular topic in the past few years, so it is rare that we schedule one of our seminars that is not close to a competitor's program. Our rule of thumb is that as long as we are not presenting on the same day and the geographic area in which we are operating has a population of at least 250,000 people, there is plenty of room for multiple programs on AD/HD. We never change our plans just because we run up against competition. For other topics for which there is less interest, this rule of thumb has to be modified.

Also keep in mind that many people attend seminars because of strong personal needs. They may be just as likely to attend your program even if they just attended a competitor's program.

BACK-OF-THE-ROOM SALES

There is additional income to be earned from selling material that will interest your seminar audiences. The most obvious items to offer for sale are books and tapes or other closely related material that addresses the topic in a different way than you do or supplements your presentation. We are careful to never withhold information that would ordinarily be part of our presentation simply because we think we can sell it in a different format to a captive audience. That would break our contract with our audience. They registered for a complete package, and it is wrong to change the rules after they have paid to attend. Material for sale must be supplemental or approach the issue from a different perspective.

At our AD/HD programs, which focus on children, we sell books on adults with AD/HD, material to help organize a student's day, story books about and for children with AD/HD, and similar material. We also offer books we have written and tapes we have prepared that contain the same content as the day's program, giving people who attend the option to buy a tape of the program they attended if they think they will want to share it with others. Back-of-the-room sales for seminars based on this book include additional references on marketing and mail order list providers, several technical books on business and accounting aspects of the seminar business, and books on public speaking, all of which supplement material presented in the seminar. We hand out material similar to that on pages 121-131 and 157-158.

Another rule we observe is to avoid pushing the material available for sale. Your audience will resent even a few minutes that are taken from their day to offer a commercial about what you have for sale. You can mention it is available, but that is it. In fact, usually someone will ask about the material in a way that allows us to speak about it for a minute or 2, but we don't push. It is your job to set the material out on a display table in a way that is attractive and draws attention. We make sure that the salesperson can answer questions about the items on sale and leave it at that. If you offer material that is interesting and useful, you will be generously rewarded.

The best way to find material to sell is to examine catalogs, consult with colleagues, and browse in bookstores. See what they have to offer. Read it. Evaluate it. Call the publisher and make a deal. Usually you can buy books from publishers at a 30% to 40% discount from the retail price. You do not have to ensure that every item you sell is of incomparable quality, but the fact that you have it on display at your program implies endorsement. Short-term profit from selling second-rate merchandise is not only ethically indefensible but is also a bad business practice. Your most profitable items will be those you produce yourself. It used to take several years before we had a good supply of our own material because we did not know what was needed and what would sell until we had presented a lot of programs, but we bring our own products to the market a lot faster now.

Just as some people are reluctant to commit the time necessary to make a project a success, there are others who underestimate the value of their own labor. When we were getting started in the seminar business, we discussed back-of-the-room book and tape sales with an experienced colleague. He presented a successful program for parents and educators dealing with learning disabilities, and he sold a number of audio cassette programs that, for the most part, featured lectures and discussions of topics presented in his seminars. He was an informative and entertaining speaker, and many of the people who attended his seminars purchased tapes, as well. In discussing the economics of producing and selling audiotapes, we learned that it cost $5 to produce a two-tape set packed in a soft plastic carry case. The retail price was $30. We thought that a 600% markup was extraordinary, but we are sure he could tell from our hesitation that we thought such an extravagant markup was excessive.

He was not insulted. He was, in fact, amused at our naïveté. "Do you think," he asked, "that people pay $30 for a few pieces of plastic? Because that's what cost me $5 - the plastic, and the tape and recording studio charges. Anyone can buy a few tapes, record a lecture, and sell them. That doesn't make them worth any more than $5 and maybe not even that. What counts is what I put on those tapes. That's what people are willing to pay for. The product, the value of what they hear, is worth $30."

We now realize that his profit was earned because he took the time to develop the material that is recorded on those tapes. He spent his own money and took the financial risk to manufacture the tapes before he knew whether he would be able to sell them for $5, let alone $30. It was an important lesson for us. We offer a variety of materials for sale. In some cases a document may consist of only a few pages but may represent hundreds of hours of research collecting information or years of our experience gained at considerable effort. And we may sell only a few copies a week or a month. When someone picks up a 25- or 50-page document and we hear them comment, "$10 is a lot of money for something that is only 25 pages long," I remember our lesson. They are not buying 25 sheets of paper, they are purchasing the value inherent in the material contained on those 25 pages and the value of that information included in the effort it took us to create the document as well as the uniqueness or scarcity of the content. You deserve fair pay for your effort.

Preparing Your Own Material for Sale

Many seminar presenters offer their own material for sale. This usually includes audio- and videotapes, books, and other printed materials. Recording companies are listed in the yellow pages. Meet with them, explain your needs, and ask to see and listen to some samples of what they have done for others. The company will be able to arrange to package your tapes as well.

Audiotapes

Tapes of the actual seminar program or tapes of supplemental material will be popular. If your audience enjoys your seminar, many will want to review what you have said, and others will want to share their experience with family or colleagues at work. Audiotapes are easy to prepare using top quality recording equipment during one of your seminars. The design of your seminar will determine how practical this is. If you are the only speaker and you have the discipline to make sure you always speak into the microphone, you should have no trouble, although the sound quality may still be poor. If, however, the program has multiple speakers or a lot of group participation that is difficult to record, you may need professional recording help.

We usually record our programs in a studio. We have better control over the quality and consistency of the program and the recording engineer is available for consultation. Depending on the length of your seminar this can be tedious, but the rewards are considerable. You will be able to reach people you could not reach in any other way and offer a useful product in a way that can be quite lucrative.

Recording studio time cost $50 to $70 an hour in 1997. It will usually take 2 hours in the studio to record an hour of your program. Advance preparation and rehearsal will keep time to a minimum and save money. Professional editing and master recording tapes will add an additional 50% to the cost. Beyond these expenses, the cost to produce the individual tapes you will offer for sale is very modest, usually less than $3 for a 60- to 90-minute tape. In larger quantities you can get tapes duplicated for as little as a dollar each.

Videotapes

Videotapes are more complex to prepare and more expensive. It currently costs approximately $5,000 to go into a studio and prepare a 3- to 4-hour seminar program for a video cassette. It is cheaper to videotape a live performance of your seminar, but the quality of such a product is difficult to maintain. In addition, very few people have the patience to sit and watch a "talking head" for hours on end. So if you tape a live presentation, it is best to do so with two cameras. While one is focused on the speaker, front and center, the other is available to record other angles or shots. Then these two tapes can be edited into a final product. If the tape is recorded in a studio, the director will use two or even three cameras. The director will vary the shots, and there will be less need for expensive editing. Nonetheless, the whole project remains a costly one. Less expensive is a shorter version of the seminar, say in the neighborhood of an hour or so. You can also prepare short programs that supplement the seminar, such as clinical illustrations, interviews with patients, demonstrations of an exercise, school behavior management programs, or an example of dealing with a noncompliant patient.

Books

Writing a book requires a substantial commitment and a lot of patience. It is also a time-consuming process that does not end when you turn over the final draft of your manuscript to the publisher. There are editorial changes, additions, copy editing, and proofreading, all of which may consume a full year before you see your book in print. If you choose to prepare a smaller publication, for example a 25-page pamphlet or booklet, most business printing companies will be able to help you design the cover and print the booklet for a reasonable cost.

If you are not already a published writer, you will find it necessary to write a number of publishers and present a proposal for your book. The proposal should include some background about your project, what the book will be about, and an explanation of why you think there is a market for your book. Send an outline or chapter synopsis and a sample chapter or two if you have already written them. *Writer's Market* (Garvey, 1995), available in any bookstore or library, provides extensive guidelines for proposal writing, as well as names of book publishers and descriptions of the types of books they are seeking.

As an alternative, you might want to publish the book yourself. This is referred to as subsidy publishing because you, rather than a publisher, pay for publication of your work. Not only do you pay for the production of the book, but the subsidy publisher will turn all the books over to you, and you will be responsible for selling them. Subsidy publishers are distinct from vanity publishers. Vanity publishers also ask you to subsidize publication of your book, but they often masquerade as general publishers and charge a lot more than you would pay to produce your own book. Vanity publishers make their money from selling this service to writers rather than from selling books. Vanity publishers rarely promote books very well, and most do not have a national distribution system to get your book into stores.

There are subsidy publishers listed in *Writer's Market* (Garvey, 1995) separately from vanity publishers. Many writers have paid to publish the first few hundred copies of their own book and then been able to demonstrate to a mainstream publisher that it is a viable product, but you can also print your own book using a printer or publisher in your own city. *Writer's Market* (Garvey, 1995) is your best resource to read about the relative merits of different types of publishing, as well as a source for the names and addresses of the companies that can help you.

HOW TO DECIDE HOW MUCH TO
CHARGE FOR YOUR SEMINAR

Your seminar should return to you all the money you invested plus a reasonable profit. How much profit is reasonable? We suggest you aim first at a figure equal to what your regular employment pays for a comparable amount of time. Leave aside for the moment how much time you put in to get the seminar up and running. In subsequent efforts, you can reasonably expect to earn 150% to 200% of your usual day's income. Of course, greater profit is attainable in some circumstances, but developing a seminar, no matter how successful, is not a get-rich-quick scheme. You should be generously paid for your work, but, as in most businesses and professions, if you love your work and put your best into it, the results will reflect your commitment, and the money will take care of itself.

Many factors influence the amount you can and should charge for your seminar. Once again, we return to the reason you are offering a seminar. This is where to begin your calculations. If your purpose is solely to attract attention to your professional practice, you might want to charge only a token fee, or perhaps no fee at all, because you will be looking for as large an audience as possible. Your purpose is not to make money from the seminar; in fact, the seminar is part of your practice promotion budget. But even in this circumstance you may want to charge a modest amount of money. We present occasional 2- or 3-hour programs for a psychiatric hospital with which we are affiliated. The hospital offers these programs to the community not only as part of its community service responsibilities, but also to market the hospital and keep a high profile among people who are likely to refer patients. It's just good busniess. They charged $5 for the last program we presented and drew 800 participants. They assumed $5 would not discourage anyone because the program was intended for professionals who knew the hospital would present a credible program, so the charge was very modest. A $5 registration fee added up to $4,000 and paid for all the costs of the program, including our fee.

If your seminar is meant to promote your practice and your audience consists of patients or clients, it is usually best to make no charge at all if your goal is to fill the room with as many people as possible. But if your presentation is highly specialized, you may want to screen members of the audience somewhat. A $5 charge will not inhibit anyone who has substantial interest and will also help you recoup some of your promotional expenses, but it might discourage those who are only curious with nothing else to do. Your costs coupled with what you can afford will determine what to spend to advertise on the radio and in the newspaper, and this will also affect your decision about a registration fee.

Other factors influence what you should charge for a seminar intended to earn a profit. People expect a meeting in a large downtown hotel to cost more than a similar program held in a church basement. How much material will you provide? It is not uncommon to be given a book or the equivalent as part of a registration fee. The book is not free; everyone knows the cost is contained within the registration fee, but that should not dissuade you from buying the book at wholesale and factoring its retail price into the registration cost. Will you serve a meal? You will have to charge for it. But when all is said and done, the registration fee for your seminar will be determined most by two factors: how much you must charge to make a reasonable profit and what your competition is charging. You have to be in line with everyone else.

In general, you are more likely to get a larger turnout with a lower price, but there are many exceptions. No matter what you *want* to charge, the marketplace will put limits on what you *can* charge. Resist the temptation to undercut the typical charge for similar programs; saving $5 or $10 rarely sells a seminar. Similarly, you usually can get away with charging a few dollars more than the going rate. The simplest way to set your fee is to see what others are charging for comparable programs and price your seminar accordingly. If this gives you a figure that also provides a reasonable profit, then you are on solid ground to proceed. If your program is unique and timely, you can charge more. If no one is offering what you have and you can convince people of the benefits to be gained by attending your seminar, you deserve to charge a somewhat higher fee. Just don't get greedy.

On the other hand, you may have developed a program that fits in a niche that is well occupied, but you want to proceed because you are very interested in your topic and do not want to cede all the niche to others. In this case you will likely attract an audience. The reason there are so many already offering similar programs is that it is a topic of considerable interest to a lot of people. But you will find that you will not be able to charge as much as you could in a niche that is not as crowded.

You will not be repaid immediately for the time and effort you put into developing your seminar. Keep track of costs and all the hours spent stuffing envelopes and licking stamps, but do not look for immediate reimbursement for these indirect expenses from your first few seminars. The cost of development should be amortized or stretched over 10, or even 20, seminars; then you can get a more realistic picture of what you are earning.

Psychological Price Barriers

Everyone knows that a price of $99.98 is intended to push the cost of an item as close to $100 as possible without crossing that psychological price barrier. It remains only 2¢ beneath the barrier and is a secret to no one. But it works. Use the same strategy for your pricing. Not all prices that end in "9" or "99" represent price barriers. It is usually better to charge $49 than $50 because $50 is a barrier, but $40 is not; there's little to be gained by pricing your program at $39 instead of $40. We price our programs to avoid psychological price barriers. Do not fear odd numbers. For several years we priced one of our seminars at $66. That figure arose from the need to adjust a lower figure because of increased costs and our desire to maintain our profit level, but we did not bump the price up to $70 or $75 when circumstances did not justify it. We have always tried to keep most of our prices in the middle of what the competition was charging or even a little lower. Not much lower, but a dollar or two. That might make little sense to anyone else, and we confess we have no data that make us think it is a sound idea, but we do it because it fits for us.

NEGOTIATING FEES FOR SPONSORED PROGRAMS

Colleges and Universities

We don't want our fee for a sponsored program to scare anyone away. Our fees are based on what we think our product is worth, taking into consideration what others charge for similar programs. But we must also consider the expectations of our customers. It takes considerable effort and expense to interest a director of continuing education at a university in one of our programs to the extent that he or she calls for additional information. None of us wants to lose a prospective sale because an administrator thinks our price is too high.

Negotiating a fee, however, is a delicate matter, and we rarely do so directly. We use an alternate strategy. When asked what we charge, we explain that we do not want money alone to serve as a barrier to the university, hospital, or other sponsoring group presenting one of our programs. But we do not suggest that our fee is negotiable. We believe a negotiable fee attracts some interest initially but does not hold up well over time. Many people think they know how to drive a hard bargain, but most do not like wheeling and dealing. In addition, customers talk to each other, and you don't want people to feel they have been taken advantage of or manipulated. Furthermore, although most people will tell you that they are happy to hear your fee is negotiable, no matter what price you quote, you have introduced an element of uncertainty into your business relationship. Now your customer has to wonder whether he or she got the best deal and whether you might have taken advantage of him or her. It's just not good business in our type of work.

From the first moment of our initial contact with a sponsoring organization we work on building a good relationship. Our immediate concern is to sell a seminar, but the best customers are repeat customers, so we hope we can build a long-term relationship with many of the sponsors. We try to be as cooperative as possible. A good reputation pays off. We are often invited to repeat seminars and, in a number of cases, we have long-term relationships with continuing education departments that have hired us to present as many as 10 seminars throughout the year. Always consider the future even as you work in the present. Some universities serve only a small portion of their state while others serve the whole state; a few even have mandates to provide continuing education across an entire region of the country or, in several cases, the whole country. A good contact can yield a lot of opportunity.

In 1997 our flat fee for a full-day seminar ranged from $2,000 to $2,500. When asked to quote a price we do so directly. But we also say that we realize that most colleges and universities have very little hard money on which to build a budget. That means they are usually expected to be, at least in part, self-supporting. Consequently, we have to present our program to them in such a way that it does not place a frightening financial obligation over their heads and promises a good profit for them. If our flat fee seems too high for them, we explain that we are willing to work for a much smaller guarantee, say $200 a day plus expenses, but want to share 50-50 in any profit that might be earned. This way if the program draws only a small crowd, there will be no major expense for our fee for the department, but, because we are sharing part of the risk, we will stand to be very well paid if the program is successful. When we share in the profit, we also ask to be allowed to take a more active role in marketing decisions.

There is risk involved in doing this. We might work hard for a day and make very little money. Only you can decide whether you want to take that risk. We always take it. The reason is simple: our experience has taught us it is a smart thing to do. From 1990 to 1997 we entered into agreements with 27 colleges and universities to either share the profit or some slight variations of this arrangement. In all, 31 programs were arranged this way. In only four did we wind up getting paid less than we would have earned if paid our fixed daily fee. But that's not the whole story. In 16 cases we earned better than twice what we would have earned if paid our regular fee. In the balance, earnings were about the same.

This arrangement appeals most to administrators who have little experience with the topics of our seminars or no experience working with us. The very first time we offered such an arrangement was to a continuing studies department at a university in Mississippi. At the time our top fee for a full-day program was $1,500. We wound up earning a little over $11,000 because the program attracted nearly 700 people. As you might expect, the administrator who handed us our check invited us back on the spot to repeat the program 6 months later but wanted the second seminar on different terms, our fixed fee. We were happy to do it.

Negotiating Fees With Co-Sponsors

Working with co-sponsors requires even more flexibility and creative financial arrangements, but we still avoid quoting a lot of different fees to different groups or altering our fee if someone expresses reluctance to pay the full amount. If you are flexible, there is more than one way to get what you want. The procedure for working with continuing education departments and setting an agreement to work for a share of the profit works with some co-sponsors, but usually we have to make different arrangements. There are many ways the co-sponsorship relationship can be structured. For example, a parent and community support group for children and families with Attention-Deficit/Hyperactivity Disorder is occasionally our co-sponsor. Most of the time this means we will offer our regular program and take all the responsibility to promote it in our usual way and at the usual expense, with a few modifications offered by our contact with the support group. Their responsibility will be to help with promotion, which includes letting their members know about the program, securing local publicity, and whatever other efforts they can make such as distributing brochures to physicians and community clinic offices. On the day of the seminar, they also help with such administrative jobs as registration or selling books.

In turn, we give them a share of the seminar income. This may be a 50% share of the profit from book sales or 10% of the gross revenue. It depends on how much work they do and how effective their marketing efforts are. Another mutually rewarding way to give them a share of the seminar is to provide the co-sponsor with 20 or 25 complimentary admissions to the seminar. They can sell them to their members or the public and add some cash to their treasury. Or they can give them to parents or teachers or others in the community in order to further their own educational needs.

In negotiating fees with co-sponsors, we remain true to the fundamental principle that guides all our financial considerations: always remain alert to the most efficient and inexpensive method to deliver a first-class product. So, if a co-sponsor absorbs the cost of brochures, advertising, meeting site, and coffee break, we have very little to lose entering into a cooperative arrangement with them. You cannot always control your income (i.e., the number of people who will register for your seminar), but you can always control expenses. Monitor your costs with a fierce eye.

Pricing In-House Programs

Most of our in-house programs are offered to schools or school districts, mental health and other health care clinics, hospitals, and social service agencies. We approach the matter of fees with each of these organizations the same way we deal with everyone else, although, because there is usually no charge to participants for the program, we do not often suggest sharing a fee or income. If we encounter any resistance to our price, we have to have an alternative to suggest in order to cause matters to go forward. What we have found most effective is to help these administrators come up with ideas that they can tap for additional revenue.

Administrators or committee heads are sometimes taken aback when they hear about the fee we charge for an in-house seminar. This is because they have seen the registration fee we charge for an independent seminar, which is $60 or $70, and say to themselves, "We would probably get them over here to talk to everybody cheaper than it would cost to send a few people to the seminar." This perception is due to the fact that it is still possible to hire a speaker on almost any topic for an honorarium or a few hundred dollars. So when an administrator expects to hear you quote a fee of $200 and you quote a fee 10 times that plus travel expenses that may add another $600 to $800, his or her usual response is to hang up the phone as quickly as possible.

But that is when the selling begins. We acknowledge that this is higher than they usually spend for this sort of program and tell them how other people have handled the fee. We explain how many times several schools or school districts combine their resources. We talk about co-sponsorship with a hospital or other community agency or support groups. In short, we do not rely on either the initiative or imagination of others to come up with ways to pay for our programs. Surely, they are just as capable as we are of coming up with some of these ideas, but they do not have the same focused interest we do, so we are alert to any opportunity to set the foundation in place that will lead to an invitation to present one of our seminars.

Chapter 8
Presenting the Seminar

A lot of work has gone into getting to this point: delivery of your seminar to a live audience that has come to hear you speak. But your preparation is not over. Many new workshop/seminar leaders assume that delivery of the seminar will take care of itself. Or some assume "anyone can stand up and talk," so they give inadequate time to practice. Others, intimidated by the prospect of public speaking, choose to ignore the need to practice their delivery, hiding behind the self-deception that first-rate content alone will carry the program. These assumptions are incorrect. Delivery style and manner are every bit as important as the content of the seminar. *What* you have to say will not reach your audience if *how* you say it gets in the way.

All seminar presenters are not created equal. Some start out with advantages of poise, mellifluous voices, and commanding stage presence. But you do not have to possess great speaking ability and a glib tongue to become a good speaker. Effective public speaking is a skill that can be learned. So you must be willing to obtain honest, critical feedback about your current delivery style and then, if you are anything less than polished, you must be willing to get help with your delivery. Then practice, practice, and practice. After all, you have invested too much into your seminar to undermine your credibility through poor delivery. There is a lot of competition in the seminar field today, and you must be able to hold your own. Although you might be successful in the short term without great delivery skills, in the long term you will lose out. We have also found that the better the presentation style the larger the volume of back-of-the-room sales.

Delivery style is connected in the audience's mind with the speaker's credibility. Does the audience perceive the speaker to be credible and trustworthy? One type of credibility, ethos, is based on how you look, sound, and appear to them - in short, how you as a speaker present yourself and your material to the audience. It's absolutely subjective and probably even unfair, but it's real, so you must be aware of this phenomenon and be prepared to use it to your advantage.

No matter how good a presenter you think you are, you ought to get feedback on presentation style. Where are your weaknesses? What needs to be improved? Do you speak too rapidly at the beginning of your program? Are you missing eye contact with those in your audience sitting in the outside chairs? Is there enough vocal variety in your delivery to keep the audience interested? Are you using your visual aids effectively? Do you have a nervous mannerism of which you are not aware? Is your use of humor appropriate? These and other aspects of delivery are the details you must pay attention to if you are to be a great presenter. *Everyone* has something to work on!

Some elements of delivery style are obvious and others are not. Think about good seminars you have attended. What made them so good? Was the presenter enjoyable to listen to? Was he or she easy to follow? Did you feel as if you liked and trusted him or her? These are elements of good delivery style and are the result of hard work and practice.

STAGE FRIGHT

Before we discuss the specific components of delivery style, we must first address the phenomenon of stage fright. Absolutely everyone has stage fright to some degree. No matter how many people you have presented to, no matter how many times you have done the same presentation, and no matter how self-confident you are, it is completely normal to feel some anxiety before every seminar you conduct. As a matter of fact, for many of us a modest degree of nervousness contributes to the energy the audience will feel emanating from us. The audience just doesn't know that this energy is caused by your nerves jangling.

For most of us, stage fright consists of fears about "what if?" What if I forget a portion of my presentation? What if the audience can tell how nervous I am? What if I can't breathe? And, maybe worst of all, what if I embarrass myself in front of the audience? Leftover from school days, this is the big one, our worst fear: that we will not "look good" in front of others, in this case an entire audience of people, many of whom are knowledgeable about the seminar topic.

For most of us, anxiety or stage fright shows up in small ways. We blush. We speak a little too fast or don't breathe correctly. We insert a few "uh"s and "uhm"s as we speak. But members of the audience cannot see most of your nervousness or recognize your fears. While you may be perspiring or breathing a little too fast, audience members are almost never aware of this. While you may skip over a small portion of your introductory comments, your audience will not know it. So take some comfort from the fact that your audience will never know just how nervous you are. Also take comfort in the knowledge that the very act of speaking dissipates most nervousness. So, a minute or 2 into your presentation, you can expect to feel a great deal better.

There are a number of other things you can do to overcome stage fright:

- Breathe. Making a concentrated effort to breathe normally will also help calm you.
- Have a glass of water ready. The time it takes you to pause and drink allows a moment to collect your thoughts and find your place again if you are lost.
- Use an outline you have memorized, but don't memorize everything you want to say. This helps keep you on track

in case you wander off the topic or get lost without sounding "canned."

- Make eye contact with the entire room. Look for a friendly face in each area of the room. Then, when speaking, look for each of these faces, thereby appearing to make eye contact with the entire room. No one will know you are looking at only a few people. And by choosing friendly looking faces, you give yourself a confidence boost.

- Imagine people, as you look around the room, thinking and talking positively about your presentation and you. Imagine them as friendly, as on your side.

- Focus on your topic and the passion you have for it. Forget about yourself and your delivery when in front of the audience.

- Most important, practice realistic self-talk as opposed to negative self-talk. If you listen to your current self-talk and what you say about your upcoming presentation, and it is negative, stop. Practice telling yourself that you will be fine; you've always done well in the past, that you are the expert and people have come to hear you talk, and that you know your material and have practiced a great deal.

- Finally, practice, practice, practice. Nothing can help stage fright as much as practice. Practice out loud. Practice for other people who will be honest with you (not your mother). Join a group like Toastmasters International which has local chapters everywhere. They will give you a chance to practice in front of a live audience.

These "tricks," and others you create for yourself, will not eliminate stage fright, but they will go a long way toward helping you manage your fears.

DELIVERY COMPONENTS

Many of the things we associate with good delivery style are elements of the speaker's nonverbal and paraverbal communications. Paraverbal communication refers to sounds which have no meaning or act as fillers which we interject into conversation or a speech. They include "uhm," "uh," and other sounds as well as sighs, throat clearing, and coughs. Nonverbal communication refers to how we move, gesture, make eye contact, and dress. Research shows that when the speaker's nonverbal or paraverbal communication conflicts with what the speaker is saying, audience members tend to trust more in the nonverbal messages they are being given. For instance, a speaker who says that a new surgical procedure is very effective, while unconsciously making an anxious face or wringing his or her hands, will cause the audience to doubt his or her spoken words. Our faces, our gestures, and our bodies are what people tend to believe.

Most nonverbal communication is unconscious. We don't know what face we're making or how we're standing. As a professional seminar leader, you must become conscious of these elements of your delivery style. Practice having a pleasant look on your face. And remember that your facial expression must "match" what you are saying. Be careful of appearing happy when talking about serious or negative things. The opposite is, of course, also true. A dour face, when discussing a humorous or light story, will also cause your audience to miss your point.

Eye contact is another element of a speaker's nonverbal communication which listeners often identify as part of a successful presentation. Poor speakers will often make eye contact with only one side of the room or leave out a portion of their audience when they make eye contact. Eye contact must be made around the entire room rather than just one section of the room. Although it is not important that you, as the speaker, actually see into an individual's eyes, it is necessary that audience members believe you have looked directly at them. Another cause of inadequate eye contact is not knowing your material well enough. Be familiar enough with your material that you do not need to look down at your notes much. Participants resent a speaker who reads to them.

Your movements are critical. A rigid unmoving speaker is not very interesting for audience members to watch. On the other hand, too much movement or movement that is perceived to be a nervous mannerism is disturbing to your audience. If you like to use a podium or lectern, try to move away from it occasionally.

Use more of the floor space. This can help capture and maintain the audience's attention. Gestures, to accentuate what you are saying, are wonderful but must not be overdone to the point of being distracting to the audience. Notice what nervous mannerisms you have. Many of us swing our feet or pick at ourselves out of nervousness. Don't.

Your voice is vital to your success as a seminar leader. Speak up and project your voice, even if using a microphone. Be careful to enunciate all of your words carefully. Change in intonation is crucial to avoid monotony, a surefire turn-off for your audience. Vary the pace of speaking and the volume of your voice as well. Watch for nervousness which shows up as fillers in your speech, such as "you know," "like," or "uhm." Honest feedback will help you to identify these bothersome speech habits of which you are probably unaware.

Use language that is easily understood by your intended audience. You get no extra credit for using "ten cent" words. Avoid using words which you and others in your field use regularly, but are jargon to your audience. Also be careful when using acronyms which are not commonly understood by everyone. You may understand that an audit by the JCAH refers to the Joint Commission on Accreditation of Hospitals, but unless they have sweated through such an audit, no one else in you audience will. Some language is inflammatory. Although language is only symbolic, most of us react to certain words and phrases as if they had absolute meaning. Know your audience ahead of time and choose words which do not inflame, unless that is your intention. Also watch for regionalism or words used only by certain cultural groups. You can't possibly get your message across if no one knows what you're talking about or if you misuse jargon or colloquialisms, even if done with the best of intentions.

Effective workshop leaders are well organized. It is helpful to tell your audience at the beginning of the program what your purpose(s) for the program (is)are and the organization you have planned. Then, stick to that organization, telling your audience throughout the day where you've been, where you are, and where you're going. Use transitional words and phrases (such as, "my next point is . . ." or "in conclusion . . .") that alert audience members to changes you are making.

Pay special attention to both the beginning and the end of the program. A seminar leader who starts out strongly has gained the audience's attention and created positive expectations for the material that follows. A speaker who starts out poorly may never be able to regain the audience's attention, no matter how good he or she gets later on.

USE OF MATERIALS

Effective use of supporting materials is another element of delivery style. Audiovisual equipment is a challenge for many seminar leaders although it need not be. Whether your seminar design calls for flip charts, VCRs and monitors, audio systems, large screen projection systems, or simple overheads, hotels can almost always arrange for your rental of these items. Sophisticated computer equipment is something you will probably want to bring yourself if your design necessitates it. Either way, be certain that all your equipment is working and that you are familiar with it. Try all of your materials before the first audience member arrives. Your audience will have little patience for your learning how to work the audiovisual equipment during their workshop time.

If you intend to use any other type of visual aid, be equally sure you are prepared to use it and at the appropriate time. A visual aid that sits in view all day during the seminar and never gets used leaves a big question in the minds of attendees. Is the visual aid visible to everyone in the room? If not, forget it. Is a visual aid really called for? Will everyone understand the visual aid? If not, be ready to skip it or explain it.

Management of handouts is another often overlooked element of presentation style. Every audience, for every topic imaginable, has come to expect handouts as part of the seminar fee. You will probably not receive rave reviews for your best handout materials, but be assured that the absence of handouts, or handouts that are poor quality, will be noted by attendees. The handouts you employ should be appropriate to your topic and your seminar design. We find it easiest to give out almost all handouts at the time of registration. This avoids the time and disruption of doing this during your program. If you do distribute a handout during your program, it should be because you are going to use it right then and because a preview of the material to audience members would weaken your use of the material. Anything you hand out during the seminar is going to be looked at immediately by audience members. Allow time for this and don't try to talk over this inattention. The ineffective use of any or all of these things will greatly diminish your credibility as a speaker, and, of course, building and maintaining your credibility is exactly what all this effort is about. A smoothly running operation will not be sufficient for your audience to exclaim over you; in fact, if things run well, most people won't even notice. It is the glitches that draw attention. As with good organization of material, a seamless presentation is most noteworthy when it is invisible to the audience.

BUILDING A RELATIONSHIP WITH YOUR AUDIENCE

Much of what we have discussed so far are the tangible variables of delivery style that you must be aware of and work on. How you look, how you talk, how you handle your audience, how you organize your materials, plus a thousand other small things will go a long way toward enhancing your credibility as a seminar leader. There are a number of other intangible elements of delivery style which you must also use to enhance your credibility and, therefore, the credibility of what you say. Good seminar/workshop leaders build relationships with their audiences. This is done through building feelings of confidence and trust in you by the audience. The audience that likes and trusts you will also attribute greater credibility to you and be more accepting of your message.

How does a workshop leader build a relationship of trust and liking when facing an audience of 50, 100, 200, or even 500 people? There are several ways a presenter can build relationships in these settings, ways that are the same as those we use to build any relationship in our lives. One of the best ways to do this is to tell the audience a little bit about yourself. We all like people better when they come a little closer to us, just as we are put off by people we meet who remain distant or aloof. Most of us use self-disclosure to build relationships. We meet someone we like, whom we want to know better, and we begin to build our relationship by telling that person a little about ourselves - maybe our name, where we live, or what we do for a living. You tell a little, and then the other person tells a little, and if all goes well, you each tell more and more about yourselves. Not only does the amount of information you share in this new relationship increase, but so does the level of risk increase in what you disclose. As you accept each other, you become more comfortable and you reveal more about yourself up to the level that is appropriate for the type of relationship you are building and for the amount of disclosure you receive from the other person.

This process is both a conscious and unconscious one in the personal relationships you form and build. As a seminar leader you must make a conscious effort to self-disclose to your audience in a way that will help them like and trust you and, therefore, accept what you have to say during the seminar. Your audience will learn about you and form judgments about you based on everything we have discussed up to this point. This will also happen because of what you choose to tell them about yourself. As in any relationship, you start with the easiest and most socially acceptable information to reveal about yourself. Obvious examples include opening remarks about who you are, why you're doing this type of work, and your specific qualifications for the work. Perhaps, to illustrate the points you're making, you move on to talk about examples of your own experiences in a given area. Maybe you tell the audience something more personal about yourself, such as how you felt during the experience you've just described.

Effective self-disclosure must be appropriate to the situation, the topic, your audience, and your goals. What works for one audience and topic will not work for another. You are probably your own best judge here. Do you feel comfortable about what you want to divulge to the audience? No? Then forget it. If you were a member of this audience, would this self-disclosure help or hurt the good feelings you have for the speaker? Hurt? Again, forget it! Explaining to your audience that your professional interest in autistic youngsters is partially a result of growing up with

Chapter 8: Presenting the Seminar

an autistic sibling makes sense. Telling a somewhat humorous story from your childhood about your autistic sibling also makes sense if your goal is to provide a concrete example of a point you are making. Maybe informing your audience about your parents' conflict over this sibling also makes sense to reinforce your point about the repercussions on the family unit of raising an autistic youngster, but maybe the audience would gain just as much from a similar example from your professional practice and leave them more comfortable. And finally, details about how your parents experienced so much discord that they went through a bitter, protracted divorce that cost your father every penny he had and left your mother in therapy for 11 years and an alcoholic is definitely more than your audience would need to know or even want to know and would not further your goals one bit.

Humor can help make your points and provide some enjoyment for your audience. Some humor is great, providing it is appropriate to the topic, providing you're comfortable using it and can pull it off, and as long as you don't go to such an extreme that your workshop presentation sounds more like a standup comedy routine.

Research shows that audiences learn more from stories, anecdotes, and illustrations than straight facts and statistics. The stories help us better understand what the speaker is trying to say and also help us to retain the information longer. Therefore, some stories and examples are wonderful. Just don't eliminate all other forms of information. When in doubt, go back and reconsider what you have found most helpful in the seminars you have attended.

QUESTION AND ANSWER PERIOD

We handle questions from the audience in two ways. For half-day programs, we schedule a question period at the end of the program. For a day-long program we take questions once or twice in the morning and again in the afternoon, choosing a place to stop that does not interfere with the organized flow of seminar material. We do not want to force people to wait until the end of the day to ask questions. They get frustrated if, in an effort to keep their question in mind, they miss some of what you want them to learn. There may be isolated circumstances when you might want to take questions as they arise, but often questions take you off on a tangent where one question leads to another, many of which do not interest the rest of your audience. Always keep the other members of your audience in mind. If you have a full room and someone in the front half of the room asks a long-winded question that is not audible to the people in the back half of the room, they will not sit still and wait if they have no idea why they are sitting wasting their time. Even if you repeat the question, chances are that a majority of the audience will not care about the topic of the question.

So we stop for questions, usually when we take breaks. Many of the questions will be answered later in the program, and we tell people that and go on to the next question. We repeat the question so everyone can hear it and in many cases (more often, in fact, than not) we expand on some aspect of the question in a way that will allow us to make more general points that will interest the group as a whole, while at the same time answering the question.

For example, if we have spoken about behavior modification as a method to deal with children whose behavior is out of control someone might ask, "What do I tell my other child when she sees her sister getting these special treats?" We use the question as an opportunity to discuss the issue of treating any child differently than others, whether it is in the family or the classroom. We offer our thoughts about the effect, not just on other children, but on the child who is being treated differently, too. This gives a fair answer to the person who raises the question, but takes the issue and broadens it enough so that other people are bound to be interested.

Do not let the question period go on forever. You do not have to answer everyone's question. If you keep going until there are no more hands in the air, you will bore the rest of your audience. Questions get repetitive and tedious after a while. Answering questions can be seductive especially if the session is going well. It is nice to be the expert. It is nice to be asked things that you put a lot of time and effort into learning, and now you are getting the respect for all that work. Make sure you are meeting the needs of the audience as a whole, not your own needs or those of a few in the room.

It can be difficult to find the proper balance between giving useful answers to questions and maintaining everyone's interest. It is helpful to distinguish two types of questions: First are questions about the content of the seminar. That is, questions that ask you to clarify or amplify something you said. This also includes questions that may not be directly related to what you have spoken about but are logical extensions. If you are discussing the medical treatment of depression and have discussed medicine and its effects and someone asks whether electroconvulsive therapy affects subsequent doses of medicine, that is certainly a question that arises from the subject you have been talking about. Or if someone asks about combining two or more drugs or questions drug interactions, even though the questions may be beyond the scope of what you were talking about at the moment, the extensions of the topic suggested by the question make sense and follow logically. It is still a question about the subject of your lecture.

The other type of question is a question that refers to a specific instance, usually a case or example in the questioner's own life. Many people may be interested in the answer to the first type of question, but unless the case asked about is especially interesting or there is a particular issue or point to be emphasized, the audience will have limited tolerance for this type of question. In a case like this you are also more likely to find the question prefaced with an elaborate background story that reflects the frustration of the questioner as much as raising the issue of the question.

We find it very effective to invite people to submit written questions. They can drop them off on the speakers' podium or your desk at break or lunch. Explain that you will look them over and try to integrate as much of the information asked for into your regular presentation and then do so if you can. You do not have to answer every question in full detail. Many people will submit multiple questions and there will be a lot of overlap. You can also take some of the questions from time to time and answer them directly. You can combine them. You can see if there are topics raised by several people that suggest a slight modification in your plans for later in the day.

A few people will protest that they cannot write their question in a form brief enough to fit on a half sheet of paper or three-by-five card or even a whole sheet of paper. There may be a few exceptions, but our experience has been that anyone who cannot write a question succinctly, even if given a whole sheet of paper, will not be able to voice that question clearly, either. Usually, people who cannot submit brief written questions do not have questions; they want a consultation. We suggest that the seminar is not the forum for that.

You will also have to teach your audience to ask questions in a form that is most useful and efficient. For example, we do programs on a variety of clinical psychology topics. So the questions we get may be about the clinical topic, say depression or an eating disorder, but a good share of them are questions about a particular person. A teacher for example may want help finding ways to keep an impulsive 6-year-old from hitting or swearing in the classroom.

But we rarely get questions such as "Can you give us some ideas about how to cut down on the hitting by an impulsive 6-year-old?" Instead, we get questions that start with a case history and include a lot of information that we don't need. Even more important, the extraneous material is of absolutely no interest to anyone else in the audience. Rather than criticize or draw attention to an individual, we usually introduce the first question period with the request that individuals ask their questions as straightforwardly as possible without giving us a lot of background information. If we need more information to offer a clear answer, we will ask for it. That will frustrate a small number of the members of your audience but will please the majority.

HOW TO HANDLE PROVOCATIVE OR ARGUMENTATIVE QUESTIONS OR COMMENTS

Occasionally someone in the audience will want to make a comment instead of ask a question. We usually have no objection because most of the time the comments are interesting. Most common is a comment that amplifies one of our responses or offers a personal experience to confirm or extend something that has been discussed. Comments that are argumentative or intended to prove you or other members of the audience are wrong are less common, but they occur often enough to create awkward moments if you allow them. This is not to say that nothing good can come of a challenge or disagreement. You do not lose your credibility by showing your audience that you are open to the opinions of others, but every once in a while a person in the audience becomes angry with something you have said or feels so misunderstood in their interactions with others that it is not enough to let them have the floor for a moment. They want to go on and on or insist on an argument. This type of behavior has to be controlled before it causes problems.

There is no place in a seminar for caustic or aggressive responses, even if your response quiets an annoying member of the audience. You are the leader in the room, and most people see this type of response as bullying or arrogant. The most effective way to deal with such an interruption is to let the person speak for a minute or 2 at the most and then interrupt to respond. Acknowledge the legitimacy of the questioner's comments even if you have to bite your tongue not to call it all rubbish. Rephrase or reframe the issue by grabbing hold of one element of what the speaker mentioned and bring it back to your main point which you can reiterate with another example or other evidence in support of your point of view. Then move quickly to another questioner or continue your lecture. Do not give the person another chance to speak.

If, as happens on rare occasions, this member of the audience interrupts or tries to intrude on the next segment of your program, agree that he or she has raised an interesting issue and tell him or her you would be happy to talk to him or her privately during the break, but that in the interest of everyone else you want to move on.

A FINAL WORD

No matter how well you prepare, some things are bound to go wrong during your presentation. There are only so many things you can prepare for ahead of time. Knowing your design and your material well is essential. So are practice and realistic self-talk when facing stage fright. Arriving early the day of the seminar to practice using the equipment is also smart. This will also allow you to make certain your room is set up as you requested and all of your material has been delivered as requested.

Our final word of advice on delivery is to relax and enjoy yourself. You've no doubt done everything you can - now have fun. Nothing will enhance your credibility with your audience as much as letting them see that you are enjoying yourself.

Chapter 9

What's Keeping You From Doing It?

Almost everyone who has read this book has given some thought to developing a seminar long before they came across this text. In fact, many readers have probably given a lot of thought to seminars. We know about the frustration some of you have experienced because we have seen how others have felt when they failed to capitalize on their own good ideas.

Why does it happen? What keeps otherwise ambitious and hardworking professional men and women from following through on their ideas? We have no doubt that the content of this book will provide a great deal of help for many people. But we also know that before you ever read a single chapter, you had enough common sense to at least get started and give it a try. Why didn't you?

It cannot be that it is too expensive. We have shown that it is not. It cannot be that it is so difficult to come up with a marketable idea; we have shown that it isn't. It cannot be that the knowledge of booking meeting rooms or designing promotional materials is too arcane or is beyond the ability of the average professional. We have shown that it isn't.

A few people are ambivalent. Their indecision reflects a tentative commitment, so they wax and wane in their level of enthusiasm. For others, the enthusiasm is there but is accompanied by a reluctance to take the risks necessary, both financial and personal. If you think you have the idea of a lifetime, it takes quite a bit of courage to expose your proposal to public scrutiny and run the risk that no one shares your enthusiasm.

If you say that you have not had the time to start a seminar project, we don't have to tell you that you are fooling yourself. We bet you know that already. It is a convenient excuse, one that most of us will let ourselves get away with on occasion, but we would never tolerate the same excuse from a patient or executive in a business where we are consulting.

Understanding why you have not proceeded further in developing your seminar is an important step to ensure that you will now be able to move forward from what you have learned in this book to a project of your own. Developing and setting up a seminar probably sounds like a lot of work. Of course it is. If it were easy, everybody would do it. Excellence in any area of endeavor does not come cheap in terms of time, effort, or commitment. But if you have the ideas and, most importantly in this context, you have the dream, it is time for self-assessment that will help you recognize your excuses for what they are and meet them forthrightly.

For most people, the answer to the question about why they have not already started is a complex one. It is usually a blend of self-doubt mixed with a healthy dose of ignorance about the processes and what is involved in developing and presenting a seminar. The latter is a topic we have tried to make manageable with this book. We have also tried to convey that getting into the seminar business is relatively easy, to help alleviate any self-doubt you may have.

Margaret Leonard is a 37-year-old physical therapist who has spent the last 10 years working with patients who have suffered closed head injuries. She is employed by a rehabilitation center and also works 1 day a week in a nearby acute care hospital. About 3 years ago she began to flirt with the idea of offering seminars or workshops to help other physical therapists work more effectively getting patients to adhere to their physical therapy program. She knew that this meant encouraging the patients' families to participate as well.

But she was hesitant.

"Who was I to be talking about compliance with physical therapy and other medical treatment?" she said. "Other people have written books about the subject. I haven't written anything. Why would anyone want to listen to me?"

As it turned out, people wanted to listen to her because she had a lot of useful things to say. Her enthusiasm for her topic was infectious. She was friendly and approachable. She found quite a bit of support when she talked to other physical therapists and physicians with whom she worked. They all encouraged her to get started.

So she did. She started small with a few lectures for families of patients with head injuries. She used the waiting room at the rehabilitation center in the evening. She began to advertise and sent flyers to other physical therapists and medical offices. At first she angled her programs for families and the patients themselves. Then she turned to a different focus and began training other physical therapists.

As she gained experience, Margaret found that issues related to compliance with physical therapy were not much different than compliance with other medical procedures, so she found new perspectives and new audiences. As her experience grew and her knowledge and skills coalesced, she decided she had enough material to write several articles for professional journals and lay publications.

"The funny thing is that I was always the shy one," Margaret said. "Imagine me, getting up in front of an audience. I thought I had to have the formal credentials, the publications, or an MD degree before I could get started." What is it you think you have to have before you can get started?

Margaret Leonard did it. We did it. You can do it, too.

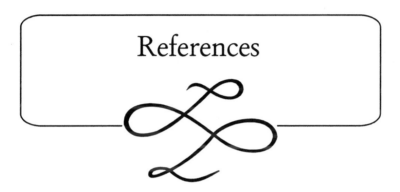

References

CITED RESOURCES

Direct Mail List Rates and Data. (1992). Wilmette, IL: Standard Rates and Data Service.

Garvey, M. (Ed.). (1995). *Writer's Market.* Cincinnati, OH: Writer's Digest Books.

Holtz, H. (1987). *Expanding Your Consulting Practice With Seminars.* New York: John Wiley & Sons.

Jaszczak, S. (Ed.). (1997). *Encyclopedia of Associations.* Detroit, MI: Gale Research.

Johnson, S. (1995, August 6). Continuing Education: College a la Carte. *New York Times* (Education Life Suppl.), pp. 22-24.

Kiechel, W., III. (1993, May 17). How we will work in the year 2000. *Fortune, 127,* 38-52.

Kremer, J. (1992). *The Complete Direct Marketing Source Book.* New York: John Wiley & Sons.

Quicken User's Manual (Version 4). (1994). Menlo Park, CA: Intuit.

Industry report. (1996, October). *Training Magazine, 33*(10), 42.
Shenson, H. L. (1990). *How to Develop & Promote Successful Seminars & Workshops.* New York: John Wiley & Sons.

ADDITIONAL READING

Burgett, G. (1993). *Niche Marketing.* Santa Maria, CA: Communications Unlimited.
Greenbaum, T. L. (1993). *The Handbook for Focus Group Research.* New York: Lexington Books.
Herman, J. (1995). *Insider's Guide to Book Editors, Publishers, and Literary Agents.* Rocklin, CA: Prima Publishing.
Holtz, H. (1985). *The Business of Public Speaking.* New York: John Wiley & Sons.
Jolles, R. L. (1993). *How to Run Seminars and Workshops.* New York: John Wiley & Sons.
Leech, T. (1993). *How to Prepare, Stage, & Deliver Winning Presentations.* New York: Amacom.
Materka, P. R. (1986). *Workshops & Seminars: Planning, Producing, and Profiting.* Englewood Cliffs, NJ: Prentice-Hall.
Pocket Pal - A Graphic Arts Production Handbook. (1995). Memphis, TN: International Paper Company.
Simerly, R. G. (1990). *Planning and Marketing Conferences and Workshops.* San Francisco: Jossey-Bass.
Zinsser, W. (1992). *On Writing Well.* New York: Harper & Row.

Subject Index

Ronald J. Friedman and Penny Altman are available to consult with you to help you develop your own seminar program. They can provide assistance with market research, topic selection and development, marketing, and program design. There is no charge for an initial consultation. The consultation program will be tailored to meet your interests and needs. For further information, write or call

Educational Development Center
8606 N. Timberlane
Scottsdale, AZ 85258

Telephone: 602-348-9084

If You Found This Book Useful . . .

You might want to know more about our other titles.

If you would like to receive our latest catalog, please return this form:

Name:_____
(Please Print)

Address:_____

Address:_____

City/State/Zip:_____
This is ❑ home ❑ office

Telephone:(_____)_____

I am a:

_____ Psychologist   _____ Mental Health Counselor
_____ Psychiatrist   _____ Marriage and Family Therapist
_____ School Psychologist   _____ Not in Mental Health Field
_____ Clinical Social Worker   _____ Other:_____

◆   ◆   ◆

Professional Resource Press
P.O. Box 15560
Sarasota, FL 34277-1560

Telephone #941-366-7913
FAX #941-366-7971
E-mail at prpress@aol.com

HDD/7/97

Add A Colleague To Our Mailing List . . .

If you would like us to send our latest catalog to one of your colleagues, please return this form.

Name:_____
(Please Print)

Address:_____

Address:_____

City/State/Zip:_____
This is ❑ home ❑ office

Telephone:(_____)_____

This person is a:

_____ Psychologist   _____ Mental Health Counselor
_____ Psychiatrist   _____ Marriage and Family Therapist
_____ School Psychologist   _____ Not in Mental Health Field
_____ Clinical Social Worker   _____ Other:_____

Name of person completing this form:_____

◆   ◆   ◆

Professional Resource Press
P.O. Box 15560
Sarasota, FL 34277-1560

Telephone #941-366-7913
FAX #941-366-7971
E-mail at prpress@aol.com

HDD/7/97